# Law Enforcement:

# Fight Against Darkness

By S. Ivan Lopes

# Table of Contents

Introduction.................................................................v

Part One .................................................................1

The Divine Pattern ....................................1

The Purpose of the Law ...........................21

New Testament Definition of Sin........................29

Saint Paul's Concept .................................34

The First Crime Scene .............................39

Describing the Chief Criminal ...........................46

Part Two .................................................................56

The War in Heaven ..................................56

Military and Paramilitary Angels........................64

Military Activity in Heaven ...................................84

Principality and Powers of Criminality................89

Resist the Criminal....................................103

The Criminal Head of State ...............................108

The War on Earth ....................................121

The Arrest of the Chief Criminal ......................128

Part Three.................................................................137

The Fall of Human Civilization .........................137

God's Unwritten Laws ...................................142

Crime and Death .................................156

The Pre-Diluvian Civilization............................169

Sodom and Gomorrah: What Caused it?............178

The Luciferian Crime.........................................188

Law and Order ..................................................204

Beliefs, Values, Virtues, and Criminality...........215

The Birth of a Criminal......................................217

Criminal Intention..............................................223

Three Groups of People ....................................228

The Value of Self-control. ................................230

Moral and Spiritual Codes ................................234

External Regulation ..........................................240

Conclusion .......................................................243

Sources............................................................251

# Introduction

This material focuses on the spiritual, moral, and social aspects of criminality. It is also of extreme relevance that we do acknowledge and honor law enforcement personnel. Those working in law enforcement are engaged in a fight against the powers of darkness. This work is established on information that the Bible provides us. Biblical history has much to say about the spirit of criminality including a description of the first crime ever committed. I understand that biblical history is not important to a great segment of society today, but that does not mean that is not important or relevant to current law enforcement and criminality.

In biblical history, police work was first performed by angels, and in some instances, angels performed certain tasks due to the absence of law enforcement as we know it today. Any biblical information regarding police work and criminality indeed catches the attention, primarily, of the police officers who are Christians. If an individual does not believe in the veracity of the Word of God, then it may have no meaning. In Heaven, the first criminal came into being. One-third of the angels in Heaven, those who had been under his command, followed Lucifer. Those angels that had been assigned to be under Lucifer's command, were part of the plan to overthrow God's Throne. There and then, criminality came into existence, and so did the spiritual powers of darkness.

I want to emphasize the fact that the existence of human civilization is highly dependent on the quality of the Code of Laws and upon the quality of its enforcement. These powers of darkness, the fallen angelic beings, are the true enemy of law enforcement. These beings hate the Code of Law. Why? Because the Code of Law's purpose is law and order; these demonic forces prefer that which is chaotic. These spiritual powers of darkness are the element influencing the mind of every individual criminal.

Criminality must be addressed as a threat to society. The work of police officers brings peace of mind to residents of the community, establishing the right conditions for the community to function in peace. People who have been born into a society in which law enforcement has been a part might incur the error of judgment, by taking the presence of law enforcement for granted. Some see law enforcement as annoying and inconvenient. Some think that police officers abuse their power, and some think that they have been prejudicial. All opinions apart, we must be sober in our thinking. We must be able to maturely determine the fact that, that which the Code of Law declares as a transgression of the law, police officers must enforce. This notion that we can write laws, but expect law enforcement to ignore them, must be rejected. If the Code of Laws has been unfairly structured, then the problem should be taken to the lawmakers, and not to law enforcement personnel. In my opinion, the Code of Law is what it needs to be in its addressing of crime, and law enforcement must do what they do best, enforce the law. Anyone having established an intention to abide by the laws of the land may feel the same way I do about law enforcement personnel, that they must enforce the law.

There are many countries in the world where the police are corrupt. Now, the fact is, here in the United States (US) a corrupt police officer would not have much of a chance. Am I being naïve? I don't think so! There are many countries in which the corruption of politicians and police officers would never be found out, but here in the US, there is a higher level of vigilance with increased chances of wrong doings being found out. Here in the US, the system is better enlightened, which facilitates wrong doings being brought to light.

One of my favorite sayings here in the United States is: "He/she is belly aching!" A lot of the complaints against the police here in the US are exactly that, belly aching! This belly aching has reached from the hallways of the US Senate to the dark allies of our cities. It seems to me that we have too many people unhappy with the United States, and this negative state of mind is being released against the officers of the law. Then, we have some very influential people working hard spending their money -- they must have plenty -- to take the sting out of the legal system of this country and give criminals more flexibility. These people argue the point that the justice system of this country has been too harsh and impartial toward some people, making them a target, and object of persecution. In the middle of it all, law enforcement has been under attack. I consider this movement against law enforcement as being a subtle revolution, and one which represents a direct attack on the integrity of this nation.

Biblical perspective establishes that law enforcement personnel are in the service of God and the service of humanity. The presence of law enforcement is necessary, and from a biblical perspective, it represents a light shining against the darkness of criminality. This causes law enforcement personnel to be under a great deal of stress, and also to become vulnerable to oppressive and depressive symptoms. Oppression is of a spiritual nature and is very common among people who interfere with the work of darkness, by proclaiming biblical principles. Law enforcement does interfere with the powers of darkness, by enforcing the Code of Law. I want to promote the idea that the Code of Law is like the Bible, and by enforcing it, the officer rightfully interferes with the perpetration of acts of transgressions, criminality, and sinfulness. In I Timothy 1:8-10, we read:

> *"But we know that the law is good if one uses it lawfully, knowing this: that the law is not made for a righteous person, but for the lawless and insubordinate, for the ungodly and for sinners, for the unholy and profane, for murderers of fathers and murderers of mothers, for manslayers, for fornicators, for sodomites, for kidnappers, for liars, for perjurers, and if there is any other thing that is contrary to sound doctrine, according to the glorious gospel of the blessed God which was committed to my trust."*

In this text, Saint Paul explains that the Code of Law is for sinners or criminals. In the Bible, they are the same. Then, the Apostle compares the Code of Law with sound doctrines and with the gospel. This is the reason the Code of Law and its enforcement agencies became a target for the profane individual. In Biblical history, police officers are servants of the Most-High God and do serve a divine purpose on earth.

Criminality is an age-old problem, and it did not start on the earth. Most people who do not have spiritual understanding, think that everything they experience on earth started on earth. This type of thinking is secularistic and incorrect. Criminality started in eternity past, and when human beings engage in the denial of that which is eternal, they must come up with their own explanation for what they experience here on earth. I say there is more to this universe than what happens here on earth. Life on earth is either influenced by the realm of darkness or by the realm of light. Man's thoughts are either illuminated or they are darkened. There is no in-between. Criminality is darkness and law enforcement is light. The realm of light is next to man, and so is the realm of darkness. Everyone determines his course of direction and what influences him, whether light or darkness.

What turns an individual into a criminal? His own choices, but also the power influencing his thoughts is of a spiritual nature. It is not difficult to create a difference between that which is light and that which is darkness. This differentiation between light and darkness is relatively easy, and all a person has to do is establish what is right and what is wrong. This difference between right and wrong is a necessity in life, and most parental education is aimed at helping the child to learn to do exactly that, to know what is right and what is wrong, and to know what authority is. This is not complicated, much to the contrary, it is very basic information. Here is an example of it: to obey the law is right, and to disobey the law is wrong. It can be compared to the need of children to obey their parents. Who in his right mind would tell a child to disobey his parents? And, who in his right mind would tell a human being to disobey the commands of a police officer? You see, these are absolutes in this life: obey your parents and obey the police. They are both established for the strengthening of human civilization. In The Book of Proverbs, we read: *"Do not move an ancient boundary stone set up by your ancestors"* (Proverbs 22:28). It seems to me that we are getting away from some very basic norms of life in society and permissive people in a position of authority are negatively contributing. Some boundaries cannot be removed, such as the relationship between parents and their children, and between the general population and the Code of Law and its enforcement.

Only the profane person damages the relationship between parents and their children, and only the profane advises people to not respect the law and those who are sworn in to enforce the law. Being profane is part of Lucifer's criminality. The Code of Law is sacred, and its enforcement is also sacred, and if law enforcement agencies appear to need more training, we don't take care of the problem by desecrating law enforcement, but by providing the needed training so their work can be improved. An attack on law enforcement is an attack on the Code of Law, and when these attacks become systematic, then the integrity of the entire society is at risk.

Criminality is sin and sin is criminality. Criminality is the lifestyle of the profane individual. Who is the profane? He is the one who couldn't care less. He is detached, distant, disloyal, distrustful, and untrustworthy. He is amoral and is therefore unable to make quality decisions. The profane is always positioned contrary to that which is sacred and has no affinity for God and the things of God.

In Heaven, criminality is strictly a spiritual problem, but here on earth, criminality is a problem with morality and spirituality, and both have to do with the integrity of humanity.

In today's society, we have the principles of morality and spirituality being attacked by two groups of people: those who are actually committing acts of crime and those who are promoting criminality. This promotion of criminality is an irresponsible political initiative, one which has been rooted within a political ideology. Such a political ideology is liberal and socialist. The followers of this political ideology believe that they have the responsibility to promote equality between people, and part of that is to make sure to water down the Code of Law, with the purpose of providing fairer justice to criminals. They remind me of the story of the individual who tried to put out a fire by throwing gasoline into it. From a biblical perspective, criminality is the result of the powers of darkness manipulating the human mind.

# PART ONE

## The Divine Pattern

There are many aspects of the human person that can be very impressive, but one of the most important is the fact that people are free agents. This aspect of the human person, probably the most impactful in his state of being, is only one side of a person that they don't know much about. In fact, free agency is the sole explanation for the presence of evil in the universe. While many blame God, free agency is the evidence behind what people are or are not. This is to say, people can be whatever they want to be, even if that state of being is a harmful one. People are law-abiding citizens, or they are lawless because of a choice they have made internally. This rule applies to most all other areas of human experience.

If you believe in God, you must know by now that all created beings are endued with free agency (or free will). All created beings, angels, and people were given the capability to observe, assess and evaluate, make a judgment, and then decide on a proper course of direction. Everything that God has created, He has created good. Regarding angelic beings and humans, He decided to invest them with the capability to choose between alternatives available. People may ask for the reasons angels and humans were given free agency, and the answer is because that is the way God wanted it to be. You may wonder, *why would God take such a risk knowing that free agency could lead the created being to choose the wrong alternative?* That is true, but God also would have to notify His creatures about the element of accountability, so that they would really take time in their consideration of the options available before selecting.

There can be no free agency without accountability. Saint Paul, in Romans 14:12, stated: *"So, then each of us shall give account of himself to God."* This particular aspect of accountability represents the highest level of, and it is a requirement of the highest level. Here, all human beings are ordained to give God an account of everything they have said and done in this life. That is the reason free agency is so important and a very serious human capability.

Criminality, and any other human initiative, has to be interpreted as the result of choices made along the way, and therefore, individuals will answer for what is in their records. If law makers were to turn prostitution into a legal activity, I still would have to take it into very serious consideration before I would engage myself in the behavior of prostitution. The reason being that a law may allow me to do something, but that law cannot force me into doing it. I, ultimately, am the one giving an account of my actions.

So, God provides mankind with free agency, and He cannot interfere with that free agency, but He has very serious expectations about how each individual must explain the manner by which they implemented their free agency, if responsibly or not. If the government can pass laws legalizing immoral types of behaviors, and you fall for it, thinking that because it is now legal, it is acceptable, then you need to know that you are responsible for that which you do. The government only knows the accountability owed to its own laws but has no idea about accountability owed toward divine determinations.

It is possible that an individual can escape the determinations or the laws of men, but no one can certainly escape the determinations of God. God has a system of His own in place. I should say that God has created a frame of existence that no man can live outside of. In that frame of existence, God has established what is legal or illegal, what is moral or immoral, and what is criminal or not, and if the law of any given nation is compliant with His determinations or not, it does not change the reality He created. Every human person is first a debtor to God and does have the moral and the spiritual responsibility to find out what He expects from each one of them. Government is secondary to all that, if not even tertiary.

If people could escape God, without any doubt, they would. The only way people can be separated from God is for God to separate Himself from them. People do have a choice, which is to abide forever with God, or to be separated forever from Him. My personal choices determine which one, whether eternal separation or eternally with Him. However, even those who have been forever separated from God, are still aware of God's existence, although no longer able to benefit from His presence or existence.

Let's come back to life on earth. Albert Ellis, founder of Rational Emotive Behavior Therapy, had a lot to say about irrational thoughts and unrealistic expectations in life. He is quoted by many as having said that "reality stinks." Yet, he himself demonstrated a great deal of irrationality by considering the concept of soul and spirit as mostly unreasonable. Anyone discarding the concept of soul and spirit has now become unreasonable himself and is indeed even delusional. He has now entered the world of "make-believe," which does not exist. That is the equivalent of one trying to grab something out of the empty air or to touch and benefit from something that is not there. This is the reality or truly the unreality of people who dare to assume that God is not alive and real.

They are those who think that they can cancel God, without any further consequences.

Indeed, God has created a frame of existence, and outside of it, there is only emptiness or a great vacuum in which nothing is. In Genesis 1, we have the description of God creating everything in six days, and in Hebrews 11:3 we have the six days of creation in a nutshell, and we read: *"By faith we understand that the worlds were framed by the word of God, so that the things which are seen were not made of things which are visible."* When God started speaking the worlds into existence, he had the pre-existing matrix, or model in mind. He created in the realm of the visible, or physical, that which was according to what existed in the realm of the invisible or spiritual. The invisible and spiritual are first. People can get angry about it, they can pull their own hair out, and they can scream until they are blue in the face, but there is nothing that they can do to change it. People are only the visible and finite, struggling to create an effect upon the invisible and infinite, and they are placing themselves in a situation in which they will reap only frustrations and disappointments. This must be taken by faith, and in faith, people accept it as truth.

I want to add to this thought two other texts addressing the nature of the creation of the visible world. First, let's read John 1:1-3, saying: *"In the beginning was the Word, and the Word was with God, and the Word was God. He was in the beginning with God. All things were made through Him, and without Him nothing was made that was made."* In this text, we have the Word as the agent of creation, and we have Christ as the essence of all creation. Pay special attention to the statement, *"All things were made through Him, and without Him nothing was made that was made."* Then, I want to add, as a supporting text, Colossians 1:15-17, where we read:

> *"He is the image of the invisible God, the first-born over all creation. For by Him all things were created that are in heaven and that are on earth, visible and invisible, whether thrones or dominions or principalities or powers. All things were created through Him and for Him. And He is before all things, and in Him all things consist."*

He created the visible and the invisible, and He is before all things, and He is the consistency of all things. Without Him, nothing holds together, and that includes the human person.

When dealing with the metaphysical, the physical is helpless, and when dealing with the Creator, the creature is helpless. Created beings are well capable of coming up with their own story about how they came into existence, but they will always find themselves dealing with fables, fiction, and myths, just as Saint Paul wrote to Timothy, saying:

> *"Preach the word; be prepared in season and out of season; correct, rebuke and encourage—with great patience and careful instruction. For the time will come when people will not put up with sound doctrine. Instead, to suit their own desires, they will gather around them a great number of teachers to say what their itching ears want to hear. They will turn their ears away from the truth and turn aside to myths."*

For any human being to attempt to explain his or her existence outside of God's reality, is a futile attempt, and will lead to the formulation of another myth. So, we must rely upon the records of the Holy Scriptures, taking them by faith, and in doing that, we bring ourselves back to the true reality of who we really are. I can imagine another frame, but I cannot create another frame than the one which God has designed for me. I exist within the divine frame, and so does the universe around me.

According to the dictionary, a matrix is an environment or material in which something develops, a surrounding medium or structure. They say that the matrix of human life is constructed out of free choices. The female uterus is a matrix where human life is formed. The matrix of life on earth is Heaven. So, we can say that life on earth, and the systems by which it operates, was conceived in Heaven. Heaven is the "uterus" where everything was conceived: Government, authorities, court systems with their processes of defense and prosecution, and even law enforcement, which was first performed by the angels of God. Whether we believe in biblical history or not, does not change the fact that humanity is forever linked to its place of origin.

We have a structure provided by God himself. God who is the Creator of everything also knows what the most effective way is to maintain living systems. He is the author of the idea of nations, peoples, and languages. Saint Paul states:

> "And He has made from one blood every nation of men to dwell on all the face of the earth, and has determined their pre-appointed times and the boundaries of their dwellings, so that they should seek the Lord, in the hope that they might grope for Him and find Him, though He is not far from each one of us; for in Him we live and move and have our being, as also some of your own poets have said: 'For we are also His offspring'" (Acts 17:26-28).

So, to make sure that nations and peoples could sustain themselves on the earth, He provided them with a structure of government, authority, languages, court systems, and a concept of legality, so that morality be regulated. Of these, the legal code is mostly essential because everything that is accomplished on the earth must be legal. Court systems, government systems, and all other human affairs must be according to law, and all must be accomplished with justice and fairness for all. King David, regarding government, said this: *"The God of Israel said, the Rock of Israel spoke to me: He who rules over men must be just, ruling in the fear of God. And he shall be like the light of the morning when the sun rises, a morning without clouds, like the tender grass springing out of the earth, by clear shining after rain"* (II Samuel 23:3-4). What David describes here is government after the divine pattern. This is a legal government, one which is fair and just, and that cooperates for the welfare of the people.

There have been two nations in the history of mankind, which had their beginnings established according to divine principles, and both of these nations were established upon a strong Code of Law. The first one was the nation of Israel which had a theocratic form of government, and was given the Ten Commandments, (See Exodus 20:1-17). With the destruction of the nation of Israel in 70 A. D., by the Roman Empire, it took another 1700 years before another nation would be established according to divine principles: The United States of

America. The United States has been known as a nation of laws, with one of the principal values of the American People being the Law of the Land.

America, as a land of law, is under attack, and so are its law enforcement agencies. Why? Because darkness is trying to take over. If the Code of Law is crippled, darkness will make its advancements. The powers of darkness are active on the earth and have in the minds of people, its main field of action. Criminality may start with circumstantial, sporadic thoughts, but in time and without proper intervention, it becomes a mind-set. Law enforcement, in making an arrest, could prove to be an intervention that may positively affect a person's life forever. Man does not create anything. He can be inventive, but he is not creative. Man has a powerful imagination, and we usually refer to an individual who is imaginative as being creative, but he is only operating within a system created by God Himself. Humanity is unable to escape the reality of God, some even try, but do not know that they are only being delusional. Why are they delusional? Because God is humanity's true reality, and He is their true enabler. Without God we have nothing, and we are nothing. Without Him, we find ourselves to be incomplete and unable to achieve personal fulfillment.

Take languages for example, which we have developed, but not created or invented. Language is a

God-given aptitude. At one time, all there was on the earth was one language, as we read in Genesis 11:1, saying: *"Now the whole world had one language and a common speech."* The multiplicity of languages surfaced at the Tower of Babel. This is what it is declared to us in Genesis 1:6-7, *"The Lord said, "If as one people speaking the same language, they have begun to do this, then nothing they plan to do will be impossible for them. Come, let us go down and confuse their language so they will not understand each other."* So, we can say that out of confusion, God provoked a state of social confusion, and the plurality of languages started to progressively surface from the depths of the human soul, thus coming into reality. In Genesis 11:9, we read: *"That is why it was called Babel—because there the Lord confused the language of the whole world. From there the Lord scattered them over the face of the whole earth."*

People did not have to go to school, or study languages by reading books, they simply found themselves speaking it, and all those who could understand each other developed their own communities, which in time became nations. And, if they did not have to go to school or read books to learn these languages, then how did it come about? By divine endowment. Language is one of the human potentials which is inherent in the human soul. So, languages do exist in the reality of God's very own being. When people speak, they are only expressing the reality of the being of God.

Go ahead, and deny God, if you can. It would be a thousand times easier to deny ourselves than to deny God. God simply is! Saint Paul had a beautiful way of stating our dependence on God, by saying:

> *"The God who made the world and everything in it is the Lord of heaven and earth and does not live in temples built by human hands. And he is not served by human hands, as if he needed anything. Rather, he himself gives everyone life and breath and everything else. From one man he made all the nations, that they should inhabit the whole earth; and he marked out their appointed times in history and the boundaries of their lands. God did this so that they would seek him and perhaps reach out for him and find him, though he is not far from any one of us. 'For in him we live and move and have our being.' As some of your own poets have said, 'We are his offspring"* (Acts 17:24-28).

The human soul is the seat of all human potential, and all human potential is a gift from God, the Creator. Masonry, carpentry, sculpting, music, artisanship, etc., are all inherent to the human soul. Man discovered electricity, but the capability to think and to develop mechanisms that could allow him to release electrical power came from within him and had been contained within him from the very beginning of time. God is the source of everything, and He is the true provider, and if He was to snap his fingers and stop the flow of life to this world, humanity would cease being, going into complete darkness.

Man has a source, but his source is not humanistic, it is divine. It is a part of his inner frame, and that includes a sense of morality and spirituality. When God gave Moses the Ten Commandments, He was only writing in tablets of stone, that which he had placed within man during the process of creation. Saint Paul explains that in Romans 1:18-20, saying:

> *"The wrath of God is being revealed from heaven against all the godlessness and wickedness of people, who suppress the truth by their wickedness, since what may be known about God is plain to them, because God has made it plain to them. For since the creation of the world God's invisible qualities—his eternal power and divine nature—have been clearly seen, being understood from what has been made, so that people are without excuse."*

People are trapped within themselves, and there are a lot of people running away from their inner reality. As Saint Paul points out, some are suppressing the truth which they deny possessing. People know God, and they carry His sense of morality and spirituality, and no human law can overpower that. People know what is right and what is wrong if they only listen to themselves. In Genesis 1:26-27, it is declared to us what happened in the very beginning, saying:

> *"Then God said, "Let us make mankind in our image, in our likeness, so that they may rule over the fish in the sea and the birds in the sky, over the livestock and all the wild animals, and over all the creatures that move along the ground."*
>
> *So, God created mankind in his own image, in the image of God he created them; male and female he created them."*

In the image He provided mankind with, He established his eternal principles, and in the likeness, He reflected his aptitudes, which included thoughts, emotions, volition, and speech. So, when people think, feel, will, and speak, they are expressing their divine image and likeness. When any of these are expressed outside of divine principles and purposes, they become distorted and vain. This explains how some people can make use of their innermost capabilities and achieve great things here on earth. They might become millionaires, and billionaires, and have a position of great influence, but if they are operating outside of God, they will never be able to experience true happiness. They will always find themselves feeling like something is missing.

Mankind has not conceived the idea of government, and they have not conceived authority, but have certainly expanded on both. The idea of government, I believe, has been perfected here in the United States of America. But what is it that America did differently with the idea of government? America's founding fathers decided that the most effective form of government is the one based on laws, and that is also established on biblical principles. A legal government is not oppressive. It is fair and just. The legal government takes a firm stand against criminality and dispends great efforts toward suppressing corruption. The legal government understands the importance of establishing an efficient law enforcement agency. It understands that unless the laws of the land are enforced, society cannot survive. In other words, America's forefathers understood that no nation on the face of the earth can be a great nation, outside of God's parameters.

Below is a representation of the biblical perspective regarding the framework by which the nations of the earth operate.

**Government:** Isaiah 9:6-7, *"For to us a child is born, to us a son is given, and the government will be on his* *shoulders.*" (6a) And verse 7a states: "*Of the greatness of his government and peace there will be no end.*"

Remember what Jesus came to earth to do, which was to become the sacrificial Lamb of God with the responsibility of going to the cross to purchase our redemption. That decision was established in Heaven in eternity past. Saint Paul referring to that said: "*Blessed be the God and Father of our Lord Jesus Christ, who has blessed us with every spiritual blessing in the heavenly places in Christ, just as He chose us in Him before the foundation of the world, that we should be holy and without blame before Him in love*" (Ephes. 1:3-4). Verse 7 states:

"*In Him we have redemption through His blood, the forgiveness of sins, according to the riches of His grace.*" This decision to send Christ to die for humanity was made in Heaven, even before the foundation of the world, and so was the decision to put the government on his shoulders. This was a legal decision, because God who has given mankind dominion over the earth and gave mankind the systems of government and authority, cannot act illegally Himself.

Daniel saw the Court in Heaven in session, and he describes it as follows:

"*I was watching in the night visions, and behold, one like the Son of Man, coming with the clouds of heaven! He came to the Ancient of Days, and they brought Him near before Him. Then to Him was given dominion and glory and a kingdom, that all peoples, nations, and languages should serve Him. His dominion is an everlasting dominion, which shall not pass away, and His kingdom the one which shall not be destroyed."* (Daniel 7:13-14).

In this one vision, Daniel saw the Ancient of Days, God the Father sitting as a Judge assigning the kingdom and dominion to Jesus Christ, here seen as the Son of Man. The reality of government, and what Isaiah describes as the government being on Jesus' shoulders was a decision done in the Court of Heaven, in eternity past. Isaiah points out that the government of Christ is eternal, while the governments of the earth are temporal. In time, all governments will be placed under Him, as Saint Paul states:

*"And what is the exceeding greatness of His power toward us who believe, according to the working of His mighty power which He worked in Christ when He raised Him from the dead and seated Him at His right hand in the heavenly places, far above all principalities and power and might and dominion, and every name that is named, not only in this age but also in that which is to come"* (Ephesians 1:19-21).

17

**Court System:** Daniel 7:26, "But the court will sit, and his power will be taken away and destroyed forever." And vs 27 states: *"Then the sovereignty, power and greatness of all the kingdoms under heaven will be handed over to the holy people of the Most High. His kingdom will be an everlasting kingdom, and all rulers will worship and obey him."*

In verse 26, the court in Heaven is seated to make a decision regarding bringing to an end the rule of the Anti-Christ here on the earth at the end of times. The government of the Anti-Christ operates outside of fairness and justice. The Anti-Christ is an outlaw, and he will for a short period serve as a worldwide dictator. He will have rule over all nations. He will cause chaos, and God will have to remove him from power to re-establish law and order because criminality will have reached its most critical level at that time. God has always been profoundly interested in law and order and has done far more than people realize, to maintain law and order, in the entire universe.

**Prosecution/Accusation:** In Revelation 12:10 we read: *"Then I heard a loud voice saying in heaven, now salvation, and strength, and the kingdom of our God, and the power of His Christ have come, for the accuser of* *our brethren, who accused them before our God, day and night, has been cast down.* " In the court in Heaven, the prosecution is evil, because it wants to condemn people to eternal perdition.

**Defense or Advocacy:** In I John 2:1 we read: "*My little children, these things I write to you, so that you may not sin. And if anyone sins, we have an Advocate with the Father, Jesus Christ the righteous.* " In the court of Heaven, Satan is the element that makes a case for the condemnation of individuals, and Jesus serves as the defense lawyer.

**The Judge.** There cannot be a court system without judges. The Bible projects God as the sovereign Judge. In Genesis 18:25b, Abraham said: "Shall not the Judge of all the earth do right?" In Hebrews 12:23 reference is made to: "*...God the Judge of all.* " God serves as a Judge in the highest court of the universe. All the divine interventions on earth were the direct results of decisions made in the court in Heaven. God is committed to doing everything in a legal manner. There is no corruption in God, his integrity is perfect. God has high expectations regarding the performance of human authorities.

**Authority:** Romans 13:1b states: *"For there is no power but of God: the powers that be are ordained of God."* This is a phenomenal statement, and every human being must take it very seriously. However, God understands that human beings can take possession of the most sacred thing and give it time and they will corrupt it. This truth that there is no authority but that which has been ordained of God, should be posted on the doors of every lawmaker on the earth. Lawmakers must become aware that they have a responsibility to work toward safeguarding law and order, and that such a responsibility places them as a connection between God and all the people of the nation in which they serve.

The responsibility that lawmakers have been given, puts them in a position in which they are servants of God. The most devastating type of corruption is the corruption of lawmakers. The working of the law requires the highest level of integrity on the part of all those involved in it. Lawmakers are endowed with authority, and they must become aware that they are directly accountable to God. They must honor the law, not because of anything else, but God himself. The Code of Law is sacred and must not be dealt with profanely. Lawmakers must treat the Code of Law with reverence and honor. All these important aspects of human life were first conceived in Heaven, and God has offered them to mankind as a provision to be used, to structure life on earth. Without these elements, human civilization as we know it would come apart.

People breathe God's air, drink His water, eat the food that He provides, kill, and destroy in the attempt to get more of His gold, and then think they can kick God out of the realm of the earth. Some people dare to think they can cancel God. I say good luck to you! God is always more than just one step in front of man, for even in eternity past, he already knew that a segment of humanity was going to turn against Him, so He gave David a prophetic word in Psalm 2:1-3 saying:

> *"Why do the nations rage, And the people plot a vain thing? The kings of the earth set themselves, And the rulers take counsel together, Against the Lord and against His Anointed, saying, "Let us break their bonds in pieces and cast away their cords from us." He who sits in the heavens shall laugh; The Lord shall hold them in derision."*

And then, the Lord, desiring that they would reconsider their plan of action, mercifully provides them with a different course of direction saying: *"Kiss the Son, lest He be angry, and you perish in the way, when His wrath is kindled but a little. Blessed are all those who put their trust in Him." (Psalm 2:12).*

# The Purpose of the Law

This material is concerned with one major problem in society: criminality. This concern is the result of a current effort to restrain the field of action of police officers and to develop a more flexible approach to criminality on the part of the system of justice. I believe that the concern on the part of many public leaders is that some segments of the population have been victimized, especially by law enforcement. I think that political leaders and other prominent people are primarily concerned with the color of people's skin. Racial differences should never be the focus of attention of the law, but instead, it should always be focused on the behavior of individuals, whether it is lawful or not. Political leaders, especially, must be very careful that they don't dishonestly raise a racial issue so they can politically benefit, but at the risk of desecrating the Code of Law, and at the same time, questioning the integrity of all members of the police force. Political leaders, lawmakers, district attorneys, and prosecuting and defense lawyers, must never lose perspective of the real purpose of the law.

The purpose of the law must become the topic of discussion in every nation on the earth. Although, many nations have governments consumed by corruption and could themselves be considered criminals. Corrupt governments do very little for the people they rule over. Usually, in these nations, there is poverty and neglect toward the needs of the people, and there is no justice, no dignity dispensed, and the laws are written with a great deal of ambiguity.

The United States of America has been honorable in its efforts to make sure that human rights are respected everywhere. The United States of America has been an instrument of God in our world since its beginning. I view the US as the hope of the whole world, and if this great nation will give the rest of the world the impression that its leadership is confused about the real purpose of the law, then I see no hope for the people of the earth to be able to live in safety.

The United States of America, as a nation of laws, could be described by using the words of Jesus when He said: "*You are the light of the world. A city that is set on a hill cannot be hidden*" (Matt. 5:14). I get it, I know He is referring to believers, but I also believe that he is referring to all elements that honor God, to include a righteous nation. I consider also that the forefathers intended for this nation to be established on divine principles, one of which is its legal code; I see it as a city on the hill. Look at the Statue of Liberty, holding her burning torch up high, and that is one of the pieces of evidence of what the US means to the rest of the world. It comes with light and not darkness.

The United States of America has two elements that cause the whole world to tremble: Being a nation of laws and having an austere sense of justice. However, as an immigrant from Brazil, I fear there is a revolution going on with the purpose of fundamentally changing this nation from what it has been to something more liberal, more tolerant, and more inclusive, and yet, I find that this change cannot be made unless the nation is completely taken apart. The nation is being defaced, and I, frankly, don't like what I see taking shape right now.

One thing I see that concerns me is that there is confusion regarding the purpose of the law and its enforcement. When the integrity of the law enforcement agency is questioned, and the police are now considered to be criminals themselves, that is confusion according to the way I see it. Now, everybody knows that law enforcement here in the US is not perfect, and they also ought to know that they only enforce the laws, they don't write them. We also know that they only make arrests, but the legal process within the court system determines the outcomes, whether a conviction or not. We assume that the Department of Justice is well able to determine which officer of the law has acted to the detriment of the Code of Law, to avoid the entire law enforcement agency being placed on their heels, becoming insecure about what action to take against criminality. The position of those involved in law enforcement becomes even more complicated because, in many areas of our nation, criminals are now viewed as victims. And this is one more very critical factor to be added to the already demoralized condition of those in charge of enforcing the laws.

I see lawmakers ignoring, and even condoning illegal immigration, and yet they do nothing to change the laws. Change the laws, and let people know that our borders are open to anyone that wants to come in. If we are a nation of immigrants, which I always believed the US to be, a nation of legal immigration, but if legality does not matter, then change the laws to open-borders-kind-of-laws. In that way, the Code of Law is not mocked. Here is what bothers me: we continue to be a nation of laws, but some of our leaders are being complacent, and neglectful, preferring a *laissez-faire* approach to criminality, including illegal immigration. Law enforcement personnel are now the bad guys, and in some areas of this country, they are being hunted down by the criminals themselves, and unfortunately, to so many people, the police are only getting what they deserve! Have we, as a nation, forgotten what the purpose of the law is? Let me point out what the Apostle Paul wrote to Timothy, regarding the law. In I Timothy 1:8-10, we read:

> *"But we know that the law is good if one uses it lawfully, knowing this: that the law is not made*

*for a righteous person, but for the lawless and insubordinate, for the ungodly and for sinners, for the unholy and profane, for murderers of fathers and murderers of mothers, for manslayers, for fornicators, for sodomites, for kidnappers, for liars, for perjurers, and if there is any other thing that is contrary to sound doctrine, according to the glorious gospel of the blessed God which was committed to my trust."*

I am sure that the lawmakers know exactly what the law is for because every crime has to be fully specified and well characterized so that law enforcement personnel know exactly what to do. Now, if lawmakers do not want these laws to be enforced, including immigration laws, then why write them? But, maybe, we are confused about it. I see confusion; what type of confusion do I see? We are not sure about the purpose of the law! We cannot have two nations, one liberal and another conservative. Are we confused about our identity? I think not, but I believe we have given up on co-existing as one. I think that unless we learn to love our great America more than we love our political ideologies, we are doomed! My heart aches for the America I learned to love, even as a street boy growing up in Brazil. I am also concerned with how divided the two parties have become, and they are both rich in values, but they used to be better able to work together for the sake of the nation than they are right now. In this war of ideologies, two very important values are being attacked the most: the Code of Law and its enforcement.

The concept of two political parties is the best idea yet, but only as long as they can work in harmony. Otherwise, they are only adding to the chaos. The Border Patrol knows exactly what to do to stop the flow of illegal entry into the country if the politicians would give them the freedom to do what they do best. Our city, county, and state police are the best-trained police in the world. Our law enforcement agencies are honorable and praiseworthy. Our police know exactly what to do regarding crime prevention, and they are also capable of intervening when a crime scene arises. But the politicians need to let the police do what they have been trained to do.

The values of law enforcement, and the law of the land, should not be the concern of just one political party. Both parties ought to be equally concerned, and they should arrive at a consensus about the importance of the Code of Law and its enforcement. Police officers should not find themselves in situations in which they know what to do but are not sure that doing it, may not cost them their jobs. They need the support of the leadership at higher levels. Political figures should not be making politics with the law and its enforcement because that is not honest. Politicizing the enforcement of our laws will put at risk the lives of officers, and the lives of the lawbreakers, and it could also even jeopardize the lives of innocent people present around the crime scene. The truth is:

- The Code of the Law is sacred, and therefore it is of no value to the profane person.
- A speech on the importance and profitability of the law is applauded only by the law-abiding person, but to the profane, the law must be enforced.
- The profane thinks chaotically, and the more chaos, the better he likes it.
- To the profane/criminal person, the concept of fairness, of being loving and caring, of hugging and being hugged, means nothing to him, and he is simply unable to process these concepts emotionally and psychologically.
- To the profane/criminal individual, the family, the neighborhood, and the city park only mean one thing: how much he can benefit himself by exploiting all of them.

Law enforcement personnel are at the forefront of the battle against criminals, transgressors, and sinners, and consequently, are in a direct fight against darkness. Here is what most people don't think about, the fact that this fight against darkness imposes a great deal of stress upon the officers. In churches, those who proclaim the Word of God, fight the darkness by broadcasting biblical principles, and the officer of the law does so by enforcing the Code of Laws. However, church houses are pretty much all safe places, but not the streets and roadways of America. These can be very dangerous places for police officers. Also, many domestic violence calls could represent a very serious threat to the officer(s) on call.

## New Testament Definition of Sin

While seeking biblical information on the topic of criminality, I was very surprised that the Greek translation of sin in the English New Testament can also be used to define criminality.

- Sarx: Means flesh or carnal, referring to fallen, depraved human nature. This definition represents the very root of criminality. I am not asking the legal system to become theologians; I am just asking them to read the laws that are in place and apply them to their full extent. God, when empowering government with authority to rule, was not asking them to pray and read the Bible every day, but He was simply expecting the government to be serious and fair, and just toward all people. And, if a criminal wants to partake in the benefits of this fairness and justice, they need to become law-abiding citizens. Criminality is the decayed nature of man in action, and only God can forgive sin, but the laws of society call for moral and legal accountability. When people in positions of authority fail to hold criminals accountable for their crimes, they become neglectful, and by not respecting the law, they become lawbreakers themselves.

- Hamartia: Means to miss the mark. It is a reference to what is wicked. Human beings are not supposed to commit acts of aggression and violence toward others. They are not created to kill, steal, and destroy, and when they do, *hamartia* declares they have missed the mark or missed their real purpose in life, and the Code of Law when enforced, is the only hope they have to get back to where they belong. To facilitate things for the criminal will only serve to push him deeper into his own hell.

- Adikia: it is an act of injustice and can be also used in juridical contexts.

- Paraptoma: It means violation of the laws and denotes also a moral failure. Criminality is both an oral and spiritual problem. It is a moral and spiritual failure because the life of crime is way below expectations. Now, if a person is missing his purpose in life until he finds his purpose, he is a failure. In sin, he is a failure as a spiritual person, and in crime, he is a moral failure. Those are just the facts, and we need to have integrity in the application of the law, and we must also be truthful in our description of criminals.

- Parabasis: The transgression of violation of a given law.
- Anomos: Person without law; a transgressor of the law; lawless, wicked, and he who opposes the law. Also translated as iniquity in the New Testament text. In the biblical text, this word means a lot. The usage of this word in the New Testament defines Satan as the role model for all criminals. In fact, Saint Paul refers to him as the one who empowers the Lawless one, or the Anti-Christ. In II Thessalonians 2:7-9, we read:

*"For the mystery of lawlessness is already at work; only He who now restrains will do so until He is taken out of the way. And then the lawless one will be revealed, whom the Lord will consume with the breath of His mouth and destroy with the brightness of His coming. The coming of the lawless one is according to the working of Satan,*

*with all power, signs, and lying wonders."* The reason the Anti-Christ is referred to as the "Lawless one," is because he operates according to the spirit of criminality, which is satanic. Officers of the law are, every day, fighting darkness, and every day they are going against satanic forces. The Code of the Law is the light of the police officer, and I say, let it shine! People who are serving in the American Congress but come on National TV accusing police officers of being abusive, are themselves promoting the government of the Anti-Christ. The spirit of the antichrist has been active on the face of the earth, from the very beginning of time. Saint John exposed people who were operating inside and outside the church. We can say now that this type of spirit is active with the governments of the nations of the earth. In I John 4:1-3 we read:

*"Beloved, do not trust every spirit but test the spirits to see whether they belong to God, because many false prophets have gone out into the world. This is how you can know the Spirit of God: every spirit that acknowledges Jesus Christ come in the flesh belongs to God, and every spirit that does not acknowledge Jesus does not belong to God. This is the spirit of the antichrist that, as*

*you heard, is to come, but in fact, is already in the world.*"

Some may wonder why I bring the antichrist into the discussion. Because if the discussion is about lawlessness and criminality, then the antichrist is the personification of what that represents. People need to know that, according to biblical prophecies, there is a time coming to the earth in which lawlessness will rule the entire earth. I already see its signs, and some of the evidence of it is the demoralization of law enforcement and the contempt for the Code of Law of the United States of America. I will repeat myself by saying that our police force, in the United States, is by far the best-trained police in the entirety of the world, and if people will follow the instruction given by police officers, they will have nothing to worry about when approached by one of them.

Therefore, the Greek words above, all translated as *sin* in the English New Testament, describe the true reality of criminality. These words do not carry the intention of improving the appearance of crime or making it look worse than it is, but they simply present crime for what it really is: the sinfulness of mankind. Why is this information essential? Because nowadays, there is a movement at the higher levels of society, here in

America and abroad, which is an initiative of liberal/socialist people, having the purpose of minimizing the impact of criminality in the world. This is a globalist action. These people think they know more than God does, and they are placing themselves in the seat of God. They are committed to providing criminals with more flexibility, while they project a negative image of the police. They call this fair. They disempower the police and empower the criminal. Truthfully, they are promoting more crime/transgressions/sinfulness because they are giving criminals the idea that if they are caught by the police, they will face the minimum degree of consequences. So, the criminal becomes bold, daring, more aggressive, and more determined to commit crimes.

## Saint Paul's Concept

The Bible has a message for criminals: change your lifestyle or face the consequences of your transgressions. That message has a spiritual and moral meaning to it. The Bible, which is the word of God, also warns criminals about defying the police and specifically tells them that if they defy the police, they are going to have the full weight of the government's authority come down on them. The Bible is not shy in telling criminals they need to fear the authorities. In fact, fearing the authorities have kept many folks from breaking the laws of the land. In Romans 13:1-6, Saint Paul states:

> *"Let every soul be subject to the governing authorities. For there is no authority except from God, and the authorities that exist are appointed by God. Therefore, whoever resists the authority resists the ordinance of God, and those who resist will bring judgment on themselves. For rulers are not a terror to good works, but to evil. Do you want to be unafraid of the authority? Do what is good, and you will have praise from the same. For he is God's minister to you for good. But if you do evil, be afraid; for he does not bear the sword in vain; for he is God's minister, an avenger to execute wrath on him who practices evil. Therefore, you must be subject, not only because of wrath but also for conscience' sake. For because of this you also pay taxes, for they are God's ministers attending continually to this very thing."*

Also, in this text:

- Saint Paul addresses the standing of authority and the posture of transgressors when facing authority. In Romans 13:1-6
- All authority is from God *"there is no power but of God: the power that be are ordained of Go."*

(Romans 13:1b). The Most-High authorized government to approve laws to interfere with the perpetuation of sin/crime on the earth. Police Officers do enforce those laws.

- Paul implies that even capital punishment is possible when legally approved by the higher authority saying: *"But if thou do that which is evil, be afraid; for he bears not the sword in vain: for he is the minister of God, a revenger to execute wrath upon him that does evil* (Romans 13:4b).

- Saint Paul declares that the authority of government is: *"...for they are God's ministers, attending continually upon this very thing,"* to keep law and order on the earth thus ensuring the survival of human civilization. If the Code of Law is neglected, chaos becomes the reality which has the potential to lead to the complete disruption of society.

- Paul is warning lawmakers against becoming complacent and neglectful. Lawmakers must not underestimate the potential of criminality. This is like cancer that, if not dealt with severely and with a great deal of determination, could lead to the destruction of the whole body. Criminality has the potential to destroy entire communities.

- Romans 13:1a, states *"Let every soul be subject unto the higher powers. For there is no power but of God..."* Why establish levels of authority if these authorities are to weaken themselves by becoming neglectful in their duties, and end up losing effectiveness in dealing with crime?

So, Saint Paul speaks from a perspective that has a thorough understanding of human nature. Most police officers, by experience, also have that same insight. Police officers know that if he/she is going to be affable, then they won't be able to do their job, because the criminal will pick up on that, and then take advantage of it. What am I saying? I am saying that the police cannot do what social workers do, and neither can social workers do what the police do. There are people in government that have a notion to turn the police department into a social workers' agency. Criminality is a social problem, but not that kind of social problem. Criminality carries within its seed the drive of violence, and as it is declared in Matthew 11:12,

*"And from the days of John the Baptist until now the kingdom of heaven suffers violence, and the violent take it by force."*

The Kingdom of Heaven is a Kingdom of law and order. It has laws, sacred laws, just like the laws of the earth. The laws of the kingdom of Heaven are always being challenged, and the challenger carries violence within him, and he is always willing to kill, steal, and destroy when challenging the laws of the kingdom of Heaven, or the laws of man. Let me tell you, laws are laws, they are all sacred and holy. That is what the police officer is a guardian of. A police officer guards the sacredness and the holiness of the Code of Law.

Where did violence manifest itself first of all? In Heaven. When? In eternity past. In Ezequiel 28:16 we read: *"By the abundance of your trading You became filled with violence within, and you sinned; therefore, I cast you as a profane thing out of the mountain of God;"*

This is referring to the rebellion of the angel, Lucifer, who turned against God in Heaven and became the first criminal in the entire universe. He is the archetype of criminality, and his violence is a reference to his disregard for law and order. He disregarded and violated law and order in Heaven, and through human beings, he is doing the same thing on earth. His violence refers to the fact that he is willing to take his disdain for the law, even to the point of destroying life. He takes it by force, as he has no respect, no reverence for that which is holy and sacred. And people who have no understanding of the origin of criminality and what it represents, want the police to be nice about it. Handle criminality with kid gloves, say those who are naive!

A Motivating Factor

- Law enforcement must view themselves as representing not just the laws of human society, but also the laws of God. Fighting crime is, in the eyes of God or biblical text, the same as fighting sin.
- In the Christian church setting, sin/criminality is confronted by the preaching/teaching/proclamation of biblical principles, but out in society, sin/criminality is fought against by law enforcement personnel, when implementing the Code of Law.

## The First Crime Scene

I am not going to apologize to those people who think that the Bible is for the less intelligent person. Although, I have never seen so many intellectual individuals being such simpletons as to think that the best way for the police to deal with a crowd that is burning, looting, and vandalizing private property, is to stand down. I say that I don't need but an IQ of 45, to know better than that. So much for those who are too intellectual to take the Bible seriously. Some keep saying that here in America, we can no longer say "But the Bible says!" Again, I am not going to apologize, but instead, I want to share information from the Bible, about the onset of criminality. In Isaiah 14:12-15, we read:

> *"How you are fallen from heaven, O Lucifer, son of the morning! How you are cut down to the ground, you who weakened the nations! For you have said in your heart: 'I will ascend into heaven, I will exalt my throne above the stars of God; I will also sit on the mount of the congregation on the farthest sides of the north; I will ascend above the heights of the clouds, I will be like the Most High.' Yet you shall be brought down to Sheol, To the lowest depths of the Pit."*

The first crime committed was not on earth, but in Heaven, and was characterized by a rebellion against the throne of God and an onslaught against law and order in Heaven. This represented a cataclysmic event and generated a lot of turmoil in Heaven. Turmoil and chaos are usually the results of criminality. Heaven was not the same Heaven, because now there was a criminal on the loose. This criminal was not alone, because a third of the angels in Heaven had joined him in this act of rebellion against the Most-High God. This is why God has serious problems with criminals, and He wants them to be restrained.

In Revelation 12:4a we read: *"His tail drew a third of the stars of heaven and threw them to the earth."* This 'third of the stars are the angels that followed Lucifer, and they are commonly called *demons*. In Revelation 12:9 we are given the information about what happened to them; they were cast down to the earth, and to the earth, they brought criminality along with them,

*"So the great dragon was cast out, that serpent of old, called the Devil and Satan, who deceives the whole world; he was cast to the earth, and his angels were cast out with him."*

This text of Isaiah 14 represents the making of the first criminal ever. Saint Paul refers to him as the culprit behind every lawless initiative. When Saint Paul was writing about the antichrist, he referred to him as the "Lawless One." In II Thessalonians 2:7-9, Saint Paul states:

*"For the mystery of lawlessness is already at work; only He who now restrains will do so until He is taken out of the way. And then the <u>lawless one</u> will be revealed, whom the Lord will consume with the breath of His mouth and destroy with the brightness of His coming."*

Then, in verse 9 he presents Satan (Lucifer) as the element empowering the antichrist, saying: *"The coming of the lawless one is according to the working of Satan, with all power, signs, and lying wonders."* Satan has been working within the realm of the governments of the nations, to create a coalition of nations that will be anti-God, anti-Bible, anti-law, and anti-police. We are headed toward lawlessness, and we are seeing the beginning stages of its development. The movement to defund the police is one of those signs. Another sign is represented by publicly elected lawmakers, and yet they are anti-police and extremely affable in the combat of criminality. The development of political parties which no longer disapprove of illegal immigration is another sign. Illegal immigration must not be allowed because it can cause international chaos, and it also violates the sovereignty of the nations. The people of America expect the Border Patrol to stop those who are trying to illegally enter our nation. That is why they are called "Border Patrol." But, like always, we have the negative influence of politicians under the influence of defective socialism, causing law enforcement personnel to not be able to do that which they have been sworn in to do; to enforce the law.

So, according to Isaiah 14:12-15, Lucifer the criminal said, "*I will*," five times. Criminality is an act of will. It was so with Lucifer in Heaven, and it is so with criminal people here on earth. That is an illegal use of the will as a gift of God. You see, God cannot create robots. When He creates any being, angelic or human, he must endow them with volition. He created Lucifer as a volitional being. Yes, angels are created to obey, but that obedience to

God must be spontaneous, it cannot be coerced. What is a volitional being? It is one which can make choices and be analytical. The volitional being is capable of reasoning and can make determinations before choosing a course of action. A volitional being has a choice to be a law-abiding element or a lawless one. The police do not have a problem with law-abiding citizens, but rather with those who are the transgressors of the law. Those people calling for the defunding of the police are ignoring the fact that, if we want to have laws, we must also have the police because there will always be those people who will be acting in defiance of the Code of Law.

So, Lucifer looked around and liked what he saw. Heaven was in complete order then, but something was about to happen that would change the course of the entire universe. Lawlessness/criminality was about to rear its ugly head. Up to that time, there was no darkness in the universe. The universe was a kingdom of light, but the moment criminality was conceived in the heart of Lucifer, and then acted upon, darkness came in. This is the same darkness that law enforcement is fighting against, even today. So, he saw God and the glory of His throne, and he saw how all the angels worshipped Him, and were submissive to Him, and he thought that he was more deserving of such adoration and decided that he was going to take over.

When we think about criminality, we never imagine that Heaven would be a place where it could happen. Those people who believe in Heaven usually perceive Heaven as a place of peace, and harmony, and one where criminal behavior would never happen. For most people, Heaven and criminality are completely opposed to each other, and indeed they are. However, criminality is an act of the will, whether that be the will of angelic beings or the will of mankind. When God created angels, placing them in Heaven as their dwelling place, He was taking a risk by allowing beings, with their own volitional disposition, in Heaven. But, if God was going to create beings to serve Him, He must make sure that they will serve Him out of their response to Him. God, being God, cannot accept any other service but that which is offered to Him spontaneously. In Ezekiel 28:15, we read: *"You were perfect in your ways from the day you were created, till iniquity was found in you."* He was created perfectly, but the perfection of a created being is only a virtue for as long the creature remains faithful to its Creator. When referred to as being perfect, a creature should never be assumed to be as perfect as its Creator. So, the perfection of the creation is only conditioned to the quality of its relationship to the Creator. But in the case of Lucifer, his perfection, the fact that he was covered with precious stones (see Ezekiel 28:13), and the fact that his *"heart was lifted up because of your beauty; You corrupted your wisdom for the sake of your splendor"* (Ezek. 28:17); then in his own heart, he found himself wanting more than that which had been given to him by the Creator. It is evident that he had been given a lot more than other angels had received. So, he became prideful, ambitious, and rebellious against the Law and Order in Heaven.

This angel became delusional, and his delusion was marked by an element of grandiosity, which caused him to make a false analysis of the reality in Heaven. That is what a delusional condition does, it causes the individual to lose touch with his reality. He observed the environment around him, and in his delusional state, he said "I will" have all of this for myself. How can one be in Heaven and think he/she can take God out? How can one be on earth, and think he/she can get rid of God? You see, criminality is a delusional condition that causes individuals to falsely analyze their environment and think they can establish themselves, changing law and order for chaos, and replacing the requirements for law-abiding living with a life of transgression. It is incumbent on the police to enforce the laws and to make sure that the distorted individual perception does not prevail. But remember, the police need laws to enforce, and if the disposition of the higher level of authority is against the enforcement of certain laws, then the police will have their hands tied behind their back.

## Describing the Chief Criminal

The Bible has records of the first crime ever committed, and by whom it was committed, but it also contains information about the basic characteristics of a criminal. Social psychologists and psychologists have discussed the concept of abnormality, somewhat determining that everything is normal, depending on where you are at. So, they say that what might not be normal here, is normal somewhere else. However, I say that criminality is not normal, and by that, I mean it does not fit anywhere, except in jailhouses and prison cells. For me to say that a thief, a rapist, a physically assaultive person, a perpetrator of domestic violence, a drug dealer, etc., should be in jail, is not a judgmental attitude, but it is common sense. Because my perception of them, and my opinion about what should happen to them is not my own, but it has been inserted in the Code of Law by lawmakers themselves. Human society has made that determination, and that is the will of the people. For us, as a society, to place police officers out in the streets and expect them to not enforce the Code of Law, is non-sensical, to say the least.

When I say, I want criminals in jail, I am not acting out of hatred, I am not being racist, and acting out of prejudice, I am simply expressing that which should be the mindset of any normal human being. When I say some criminals must be taken off the streets, I am not thinking black, white, yellow, or red, I am just verbalizing a notion that has been common everywhere and by every human who considers him/herself to be a law-abiding citizen. The people who want to sleep in peace at night, and desire to walk down our streets in safety. We want our children to be safe when walking to and from school, and we want our children to play out in the park in safety. We need the police patrolling our cities, our streets, and our public playgrounds, and the people want them to do their jobs. We want our law enforcement officers to deal with criminality whether it be white, black, red, or yellow. Now, is that asking for too much? I think not!

A criminal is someone whose intentions are evil. To one degree or another, his intentions are evil. His intentions are determined by the type of character he has. Is this dooming the criminal? Absolutely not! If any criminal wants to change himself and improve the type of person he is, he can ask for help, society has plenty of resources available! So, he has an option, and he has a much better option than the commission of a crime, which is to seek help. How far down the road of criminality he wants to travel is up to him to decide, but as long as he persists in living a life of criminality, law enforcement has to do their job and must have a strong determination to be in the criminal's way.

The archetype of criminality is the role model for all criminals. Although he has been allowed to come to earth, he and his fallen angels do inhabit the realm around the earth. Saint Paul explains that in Ephesians 6:12, saying: *"For we do not wrestle against flesh and blood, but against principalities, against powers, against the rulers of the darkness of this age, against spiritual hosts of wickedness in the heavenly places."* They inhabit the air space around the globe, and their business is to influence human beings. Their influence when exerted on anyone causes thoughts and internal dispositions that will either lead to disobedience to God or disobedience to the laws of the land and in most cases, it is both. Police officers are always battling against that darkness. By being on the front line of the battle against criminality, officers of the law are always battling directly *"against principalities, against powers, against the rulers of the darkness of this age, against spiritual hosts of wickedness in the heavenly places."*

This is one reason many police officers are depressed and highly stressed. When officers of the law make use of the Code of Law and interfere with the work of these principalities and powers, they will find much resistance from this darkness. This resistance can manifest itself in the form of emotional problems, insomnia, and other types of mood disorders. Many police officers could benefit from talking to a police chaplain. They must learn the importance of:

1) praying, asking for God's protection before going on duty. And 2) they must believe that God has guardian angels watching over them.

When district attorneys, judges, and defense, and prosecuting lawyers lack spiritual understanding regarding the work of the criminal spirits, they need to remain faithful to the Code of Law because in it they have their light. If the Code of Law starts to be tampered with, then the door is open for the invasion of darkness. An invasion of darkness means an increase in crime being committed across the Nation.

So, Jesus talks about the chief criminal, and in the Gospel of John 10:1-2, he starts by creating a distinction between Himself and Satan, saying: *"Most assuredly, I say to you, he who does not enter the sheepfold by the door, but climbs up some other way, the same is a thief and a robber. But he who enters but the door is the shepherd of the sheep."* Jesus is giving us a description of the behavior of the criminal. Always coming in through the back door, using dark alleys and dark streets, always trying to sneak in furtively. The words *"thief and robber,"* as used by Jesus Christ, is a clear indication of the intentions of the spiritual criminal. Many judges, district attorneys, and defense, and prosecuting lawyers are unaware of the influence that this archetype of criminality exerts over people. That is the reason why they need to faithfully follow the Code of Law.

When people in a position of authority start asking for a revision of the justice system, it is always because they think that the Code of Law has been too strict and unfair. These politicians are always against legal ideas that aim at narrowing down the scope of action of criminals. I call that defective socialism because it is preoccupied with improving quality of life, and yet, it seeks to be implemented by facilitating wrongdoing. The Code of Law has to be harsh and restrictive, and it can only be merciful to a minimum degree, otherwise, it loses objectivity by becoming inefficient. In John 10:10, Jesus states: *"The thief does not come except to steal, and to kill, and to destroy. I have come that they may have life, and that they may have it more abundantly."* To steal, kill and destroy is what the thief (the criminal) comes in for. These three elements represent the heartbeat of criminality, and all other crime is related to it. Criminality carries an attitude of destruction; it has the potential to destroy material things (vandalism), and human life, such as aggression, violence, and homicidal acts.

The distinction that Jesus created between Him and this chief criminal, is very important. Jesus wanted to make sure he provided humanity with a brief profile of himself and Satan. In this description, Jesus was simply pointing out that He is a law-abiding citizen, but that Satan is the outlaw. He is a lawbreaker, a transgressor, and profane. Jesus said He comes to give life, to bless, to help people, but Satan comes as a criminal, as such he kills, he destroys, and he steals.

This master criminal is also described in the Book of Ezekiel, where we read: *"You were perfect in your ways from the day you were created, till iniquity was found in you"* (Ezek. 28:15). The term iniquity means lawlessness. It says he was a perfect being, but then he changed internally, and this change was not provoked by God, but by Lucifer's own cogitations. The expression "till iniquity was found in you," gives the idea that lawlessness was conceived within him, and by his own determinations. It was an act of his will. In Ezekiel 28:16, we read:

> *"By the abundance of your trading You became filled with violence within,*
> *And you sinned; Therefore, I cast you as a profane thing Out of the mountain of God;*
> *And I destroyed you, O covering cherub, From the midst of the fiery stones."*

Here we are told that this angel became filled with violence, and was removed from his position of glory, as a profane being.

The reference to violence within the criminal type varies in degrees. That is when a thief is trying to take something that does not belong to him, he is minimally acting violently because he is taking something against someone else's will. Therefore, the act of violence starts at the level at which one violates another person's will. The degree of violence will intensify to those acts of robbery in which the thief is fully aware and willing to take someone's life to get what he wants. That is why the use of police force will also vary when dealing with different criminal types. The devil is a violent being, he was not always like that, but his contempt for the Law of God, his contempt for law and order, his selfish motives, his ambitious desires, wanting something that did not belong to him, led him into becoming a usurper, and profane being.

The profane person is the one without any affinity. This type does not care much for anything, including family ties, true friendship, the value of work, religion, faith, God, and the Code of Law. The profane person has his own view of the world, and he is marked by some degree of delusion because the reality he perceives is not that of the rest of society. The profane person is destitute of values and virtues. Again, the profane person is not doomed yet, there is help in a process called rehabilitation, but if the grips of the justice system are loosened up, then his doom is a bit closer than expected.

Crime must be fought against consistently and very diligently. Those individuals who can serve in the offices of County District Attorney, or as State Attorney General, should not be elected if they have the intention of being affable in dealing with criminals. Criminals are not to be helped by receiving lesser penalties for their crimes, but instead, must be made to pay for their crimes, and this is the only way to help them, so they are forced to reconsider what their responsibilities are in society. In Matthew 24:12, Jesus stated that criminality will increase, saying: *"And because lawlessness will abound, the love of many will grow cold."*

This is not the time to assume we don't need the police. However, there has always been a segment of society that has tried to live in direct opposition to God and the Code of Laws. Unless those individuals who work for the justice system take a punitive approach to combat crime, they will only be cooperating with the increase of crime on our streets. Criminals do not need to be motivated, but I am sure that all criminals are appreciative of any break they can get!

I am afraid that the political ideology that is opposing God and the Bible, also favors criminality. They have taken on themselves the task of helping and rescuing those people who feel that the Bible is ostracizing them, and that includes criminals. Imagine now, a segment of God's creation trying to serve as the protectors of other members of creation, safeguarding them from the expectations of their Creator. After all, if those who believe in God are considered to be deplorable, bigots, homophobic, suffering from gayphobia, or lesbophobia, heterosexist, racist, etc., then that is what God Himself must be. So, they say, let's gang up against Him, and let's refuse His ideas on how people should live their lives. Let's support people in living the kind of life they want to live. Whatever they want to do, however they want to do it, and that is what we are going to support, and that includes even the criminals. They have established that if the Bible condemns it, they are going to approve, and if the Bible is against it, they are certainly going to be in favor of it. And, in the implementation of their ideology, they don't really care if crime proliferates. If the Bible is supportive of law enforcement, which it is, then they will position themselves against law enforcement, and they will attempt to take law enforcement out of the picture or find ways to render it ineffective.

If we could ask God about what to do in view of increased criminality, He would say, I want more police out in the streets. God knows that a shortage of police officers will lead to an increase in unsafe homes and un-safe streets. That is the reason God provided man with authority, and the inspiration to formulate a legal code. The Bible is supportive of a legal code, and it is sup-portive of the enforcement of the laws. Biblical history shows us that no society on the face of the earth can en-dure without laws and sufficient law enforcement.

The truth is that man is nothing without God. If man will choose to exist outside of God, he will reap exact-ly what secularism presents him with, nothing before or after. That is a condition in which we see the ultimate in what hopelessness is all about.

# PART TWO

## The War in Heaven

People who believe in the reality of Heaven usually think that everything there is just wonderful. Well, it used to be until Lucifer broke the law! Then Heaven became a place where there was a need even for angelic military power. Some of the angels were given the power to police Heaven, and also to police the universe. Why? There were, and still are, criminals on the loose. Lucifer and a third of the angels God had created, became transgressors of the law. One might say, what law? The law demands that,

*"Thou shall love the Lord your God with all your heart, and with all your soul, and with all your mind"* (Matthew 22:37).

Lucifer broke the most important of all laws, and for that, he lost his place in Heaven. He lost his love for God, thus becoming God's enemy. Now, he can no longer remain in Heaven. People wonder why God did not lock him up in His prison, or why God did not destroy him. God had and has the power to do all that but remember that this angel was endowed with a will of his own, and his heart became bad, and God would have to establish the proper manner to deal with him, in the process of time. But God could not destroy Lucifer any more than He could have destroyed mankind. When God provided him with a will of his own, God knew the risks involved, but He cannot accept service from anyone unless it is done spontaneously. The same situation applies to mankind. Why put man to the test? Because man needs to prove to God and himself that he serves God out of the desire of his heart, and this partnership with God must be spontaneous. Lucifer failed in Heaven, and then man failed in the Garden of Eden.

Now, Lucifer is required to leave Heaven and to take along with him all the angels that had sided with him. But, just like a criminal, he refused, and by refusing he declared war against the powers of Heaven. Most criminals here on earth, are not going to comply of their own free will. They have to be forced into compliance with the requirements of the law, and if those defending the Code of the Law will allow them, they will fight back, and some of them will do so even to their death.

On earth, criminality is war declared against society. John, the Revelator, saw war in Heaven. The vision he had was from an event that happened in eternity past. We have no knowledge about any time frame, and all we know is that there was an event in Heaven described as a war. John describes his vision, saying:

*"And war broke out in heaven: Michael and his angels fought with the dragon; and the dragon and his angels fought, but they did not prevail, nor was a place found for them in heaven any longer. So the great dragon was cast out, the serpent of old, called the Devil and Satan, who deceives the whole world; he was cast to the earth, and his angels were cast out with him."* (Revelation 12:7-9).

We have no idea about the length of the duration of this war, but it was a war between angelic beings, and it must have been a formidable one. We also have no idea how angelic beings fight, but they do, and human beings assume that all that is happening in the universe is that which happens only within the realm of the earth, and it shows a lack of spiritual insight on their part.

People should not assume that what they know, and experience is all that there is to know and experience. We only know a small fraction of what there is to be known about ourselves and the universe around us. So, just because I don't see it or hear it, does not mean it is not happening. The reality involved in being a human person and the reality of this vast universe is by far beyond the reach of the human physical senses.

Secularism, for example, wants people to believe that the here and now is all there is. But that is not a correct interpretation of life and time, within the universe of God. If we were to believe that there was nothing before the Big Bang and that there is nothing after this, whatever "this" means, we would suffer a great loss of meaning, and our explanation of what we are facing now would have to be based on a "guess." The finite man is simply unable to explain the infinite. If he tries to, he is only making a fool out of himself. The only way for the finite to grasp the infinite is through faith. Faith in what, or in whom! Faith in the best and most complete description of history ever; the Bible! Faith in who? Faith in God, the most reliable source of information ever known to mankind.

So, criminality is not a problem of the here-and-now, and it is not a problem restricted to the physical world! But primarily, it is a spiritual problem, and it first happened within eternity past. Someone might say, give me some evidence of that, and the answer is: take it on faith, or come up with your own story. Man can, and man has come up with his story. It takes common people to believe man but to believe God takes people of faith, and that is not common. So, God conceived the idea of authority, and He also conceived the idea of the Code of Law, and the reason

He did so was so that mankind would have the means necessary to effectively deal with criminals and criminality. If the governments of the earth become complacent toward the Code of Law, and complacent also toward the enforcement of the Legal Code, then total chaos will be the result. The type of chaos that unrestrained criminality can bring about can lead to the destruction of human civilization. It has in the past, and if the governments of the nations will insist on assuming they know best, thus rejecting divine information, the deterioration of morality is inevitable, and with that, destruction will come.

The United States must become a role model to all other nations. Who said so? Well, it comes with the idea of being the world leader. But who said so? Those who claim that the US is a world-leading nation. And, if God indeed rules in the affairs of mankind, then God also said so. In Daniel 4:17, we read:

*"This decision is by the decree of the watchers, and the sentence by the word of the holy ones, in order that the living may know that the Most High rules in the kingdom of men, gives it to whomever He will, and sets over it the lowest of men."*

If this is true, which I believe it is, and God does rule in the affairs of mankind, then He also established the United States as the leading nation for this particular period of time in human history. This brings a great deal of responsibility for American lawmakers, and it places the government of this nation in a very important spot, requiring of them the highest level of investment in dictating the pace of human progress around the globe.

In this leading role, the US government cannot afford to be either too conservative or too liberal. Extremes are never the most intelligent of approaches. I believe they have a defective socialistic idea, in that they do embrace the elements of lawlessness, in disregard to the elements of lawfulness. A defective socialistic idea is that which is implemented to improve social life, and yet, it comes for its ruin, such as the increase of perpetration of crimes in our streets and the increase of immorality.

The US Government does not have to try to reinvent the wheel! Just follow the idea of the forefathers by honoring the Judeo-Christian Code of Law. But that is exactly what the extreme liberals are against. That is the justice system they want to revise.

The US political system has to be very careful if God indeed established America as the leading nation of the world so that they do not find themselves in direct opposition to God Himself.

In the Book of Daniel 2:21, we read:

*"And He changes the times and the seasons; He removes kings and raises up kings; He gives wisdom to the wise and knowledge to those who have understanding."*

If He removes kings and raises up kings, then that also means that He raises up nations, and removes them. The US political system should know that they are accountable to God, even beyond being accountable to each other.

In addition to not being in direct opposition to God, there are a few other areas that I would consider as being huge red flags, and I list them as follows:

- Do not get the idea that you can create rules and regulations that are above and better than the divine standards.

- Do not think that you can place yourselves above God and end up legalizing human behaviors that God Himself does not allow. In other words, you make moral that which God considers to be immoral.

- You have to be careful that you do not validate behaviors, that in the end will cost people the eternity of their souls. A world-leading nation has never been given that kind of power. Great nations have been given authority and a Code of Law, but they were never given redemptive power. This has been a mistake committed by many nations, that their political power made use of written laws, to establish their political ideologies. They have the authority to do so, but if they happen to be ruling against the determinations of the Most High God, then those thinking that these laws legitimize their immorality will stand in need of atonement. And atonement, the Code of Law cannot provide. And who is going to answer for the integrity of their souls, is a question to be asked here.

- The politicians legislating to establish their own political ideology, if they are legislating extreme liberality, then a large segment of people living under their domain, will end up negatively affected. Just because a human initiative is legitimized, does not mean that God approves of it. No lawmaker on earth can prove God wrong, just by writing laws. Written laws that legitimize immorality are Luciferian.

- The US Government has a responsibility to lead politically, economically, and morally. The US must give the example of a nation that is righteous in the sight of God and in that way serve as a role model to other nations. To do that, all the US Government has to do is to honor the Code of Law, as established by the forefathers.

Lucifer was expelled from Heaven and cast down to the earth, and here the fight against criminality goes on. No nation on the face of the earth is expected to operate like a church, that is not the expectation that God has, but each nation must take a serious position against criminality. The action that serves the purpose of curbing crime, also serves the purpose of limiting Lucifer's activities on the earth, until he is also completely removed from here.

## Military and Paramilitary Angels

When Heaven was a complete paradise, there was no need for military, or even paramilitary angels. However, after the birth of criminality, law and order in Heaven came under attack. With the state of law and order threatened, the need for a military and paramilitary force became a necessity. Lucifer, or Satan, had an army of fallen demons with him. If left alone, they would continue to wage war against the Throne of God. So, we can say also that the first guerrilla warfare happened in Heaven. Imagine that! Heaven of all places! Criminality has to be taken seriously, and when a criminal resists the police on the earth, this same lawbreaker must be physically restrained at all costs. The police are always right when dealing with resistant criminals. Mothers and fathers, if you don't want your boys to be dealt with by the police, teach them to be law-abiding citizens, and to obey the authorities. It is that simple!

Only the law is fully legal, and only that which is fully legal can pass the test of the law.

The heart of criminality beats toward the resistance of authorities. Criminals do not acknowledge submission; the day they insert submission into their way of thinking, they will no longer act criminally. That spirit, or attitude of resistance is what police officers have to deal with every day. If an officer of the law takes one single step back, he will be run over. Law enforcement personnel cannot afford to be affable! They must leave affability for those in more comfortable positions of authority. Affability may cost an officer of the law his life. At the highest level of his intensity, a criminal has the potential to commit murder. You see, you don't want your children to grow up and be criminals, and maybe, just maybe, you don't want them to become police officers either. But thank God, we still have some brave men and women willing to serve society as officers of the law.

Lucifer, the archetype of criminality, must leave Heaven, but since he refuses to leave peacefully, he has to be driven out by the angels of God. And there was war in Heaven, but according to the vision described by Saint John, Lucifer, and his angels lost the war, and law and order were finally restored. Now, earth is where the turmoil is. Why earth? Because the Bible talks about two places of great importance in this universe: Heaven is one, and earth is the other. Jesus Christ points that out by saying in Matthew 5:34-35,

*"But I say to you, do not swear at all: neither by Heaven, for it is God's throne; nor by the earth, for it is His footstool;"*

Lucifer probably thought that since he could no longer remain in Heaven, he would bring his fight against God to earth, and then find a way to insert his criminal spirit into the way people think, thus creating a mindset.

In a time in which there was no law enforcement as we have today, angels performed duties that are today performed by the police. In ancient times, the nations of the earth did not have a written legal code. They had laws, but these laws were verbally transferred. That is the reason criminality, at times, got out of hand. People should be thankful for our police force, and many, indeed, are.

In the biblical text, the first police duty was performed by angels. A guardian angel is an example of a para-military force, such as we have in Genesis 3:24, where we read,

*"So he drove out man; and he placed at the east of the garden of Eden Cherubims, and a flaming sword which turned every way, to keep the way of the tree of life."* God decided to drive man out of the Garden, because they had forfeited their right to live there, and God did not want them to come back in. When the Lord declared the Garden

of Eden off-limits, he decided to place Cherubims to keep people from getting back in. These Cherubims kept watch over the entrance of the Garden, but we are not given the length of time in which they did so.

These guardian angels do protect people also, as we read in Psalms 34:7,

*"The angel of the Lord encamps round about them that fear him, and delivers them."*

And Psalms 91:11 states:

*"For he shall give his angels charge over thee, to keep thee in all thy ways."* Although the Lord has angels assigned for the protection of people, especially believers, it is also true that the protection of individuals is the responsibility of the proper authorities. What am I saying? I am saying that it is more likely that my angel will come in a police uniform after I call 911. But it is also true that if an individual's life is at risk, the Lord will provide him protection until the police arrive. That is how the Lord intends it to be, and that is why he has provided humanity with authority and a Code of Law. The Lord has His angels prepared, but most likely for supernatural necessities only.

God gave man dominion, as stated in Genesis 1:28-30, where we read:

*"Then God blessed them, and God said to them, "Be fruitful and multiply; fill the earth and subdue it; have*

*dominion over the fish of the sea, over the birds of the air, and over every living thing that moves on the earth." And God said, "See, I have given you every herb that yields seed which is on the face of all the earth, and every tree whose fruit yields seed; to you it shall be for food. Also, to every beast of the earth, to every bird of the air, and to everything that creeps on the earth, in which there is life, I have given every green herb for food"; and it was so."*

So, God told them to be fruitful, to multiply, and to replenish the earth, and it was the same as giving them the entire earth, asking them to be in charge of everything. This dominion given to mankind, could not be fully enforced unless God gave them also the authority to implement the dominion received. The authority, once understood, led humanity to the idea of an established government.

The reason God wants a fair and just government is so that people can live in freedom, and at the same time, live in a society in which no particular individual can do as he pleases. He can do as he pleases as long as his actions do not infringe upon the rights of other people in society. So, the government establishes rules that are based on equal rights for all. When the established authorities, in any nation on the earth, fail to establish laws that can generate a sense of equality for the people, that failure will lead to an open door for chaos. Here is where I believe the United States has been a role model to all other nations. The US has established a system of government that is simply the best, and there has never been anything like it in the history of mankind. This has been a nation of values, and virtues. In the United States, the concept of freedom, equal rights, God, family, and country, and the willingness to fight for the preservation of these values, serve as an example to the whole world.

I believe that America is exactly what God intended for it to be, to serve Him a purpose, and be that one point of balance between all the nations, politically, militarily, and economically. God may still have angels doing cosmic warfare above the earth, but on earth, He needs people to take care of people, especially when it comes to the rights that people have in regard to security and peace of mind. We had once what was called Roman Peace, and today we have American Peace. That is regarding world peace, but when it comes to the safety of individuals, God plans that there be an efficient police force in every city. America has had that in place, but now I see a revolution coming up and an attempt to undo the American way. Some people are caught up in a delusional state of mind referred to as "cancel it."

The established authorities do have the power to make changes. This is a huge issue concerning the element of authority. They can change laws, they can change times, and they can even change, or try to change history. Yes, they can even defund the police, and that is why the people of America need to be very careful with who they elect to power. A government has the power to make changes whether people like it or not.

Think like this, if one night at around 1 in the morning, someone is forcing one of your windows, giving you the clear impression that someone is trying to break into your home, and you dial 911, you want the police to show up and quickly, and be efficient in providing you protection. Until the police arrive, you can pray, if you believe in prayer, He might provide you with a guardian angel to keep you safe, but the police personnel that arrives are your angels. And that's the American way! The American way determines that no particular individual should take the law into his own hands. There are laws, and there are police officers sworn in to enforce the laws, and whenever you are involved in a situation with another person that has the potential to escalate, call the police. Therefore, how necessary is the police? Extremely necessary!

If the police are called to intervene in a certain situation and the individual or individuals who were the cause for the police to be called, become resistant, then they will have to be restrained by the police. If the police do not take control of the situation, and innocent individuals

70

end up hurt or maybe even killed, then the police officers involved will be charged with negligence, which could lead to their entire police department being involved in a lawsuit. If the police will force a restraint, and the subjects are injured or even killed, as has happened many times before, the officers involved might end up losing their jobs, and even being sent to prison. So, damned if they do, and damned if they don't! And that is not fair. There has got to be a system in place enabling higher authorities to oversee the actions of a particular police officer, but one that is fair for all. If a particular individual decided to resist arrest, the police must do what needs to be done to get him into their custody. That is, they must make use of all the means they have learned of in the police academy. No particular individual ought to be given the idea that he/she can resist an arrest because that will lead to total chaos.

Here in America, outlaws have been killing lawmen from the very beginning of this nation's existence. Here in America is very common that if the law wants someone, it will have to catch him! Criminals have been running away from lawmen on foot, then on horseback, and horse-drawn vehicles, and finally, now they might attempt to escape on a motorized vehicle. Yes, sir, catch me if you can! In a country where the will of the people is very strong, and where people are initiative takers, and have the determination of self-preservation, combating criminality is not for the weak of heart. In America, nothing that is done without the element of determination will get through. In America, everything and everyone that does not have determination and is not driven by persistence is doomed to failure, and that includes law enforcement. And I say, in America, when the police are called, people do not want a social worker, they want a capable and tough police officer to show up, to handle the situation. Otherwise, why call the police?

Let me mention here again, that the only reason for military angels was and still is the presence of criminal spirits dwelling in the realm around the globe. These criminal spirits are actively working, attempting to get the greatest number of people to adhere to their fight against the kingdom of God. Saint Paul, in Ephesians 6:12, reveals that they inhabit the "darkness," meaning spiritual darkness. What is spiritual darkness? It is any and every ideology or philosophy or thought pattern that is contrary to God and His will. The belief system of darkness is not structured in the ways of God's Kingdom and is not influenced by the Code of Law. To God, any idea or action that is contrary to His holiness is a crime, and it is considered to be profane.

The safety of the entire universe is at risk with these criminals on the loose! Human beings would be terrorized if they could witness cosmic warfare. In the Book of Daniel 10:12-13, we read:

*"Then he said to me, "Do not fear, Daniel, for from the first day that you set your heart to understand, and to humble yourself before your God, your words were heard; and I have come because of your words. But the prince of the kingdom of Persia withstood me twenty-one days; and behold, Michael, one of the chief princes, came to help me, for I had been left alone there with the kings of Persia."*

This one angel tells Daniel that with the help of the Archangel Michael, he had to battle the prince of the kingdom of Persia, a reference to the powers of darkness influencing the rulers of that kingdom, and that the battle lasted twenty-one days. These types of battles happen in the realm of the metaphysical, and those restricted to the physical world are unable to observe them. I am trying to show you that the battle against darkness and criminality is by far larger than people can imagine. People openly criticizing the work of law enforcement, are only demonstrating that they are ignorant about the true nature of this problem.

The military angels fighting the spirits of darkness can also be referred to as avenging angels, as recorded in II Kings 19:35, where. We read:

*"And it came to pass that night, that the angel of the Lord went out, and smote in the camp of the Assyrians*

*a Hundred and Eighty-Five Thousand: and when they arose in the morning, behold, they were all dead."*

The Assyrians were getting ready to attack Jerusalem, and this one angel came to the rescue of the city and its inhabitants. I don't think that what this angel did was seen by anyone who could have been awake that night. The angel, a spiritual being, took action in the natural world, serving as a soldier doing battle against the military of an evil nation. The Assyrian army was criminal, illegally invading the land of Israel to bring destruction and death. So, God miraculously intervened in favor of Israel, but in this day and age, God expects nations just like the United States and its allies to intervene in favor of other nations when being invaded by foreign military power.

God has given the authority of government to all nations, but there have been several nations that have used the authority they have received, and the power of their military to invade other nations, to kill to steal and to destroy, after the example of the archetype of criminality himself, (John 10:10). When that happens, it is the responsibility of the nations which stand in the integrity of the rule of law to stop the criminal nations. The United States of America has been a good role model to other nations, regarding the freedom that all nations should experience. If all nations should remain quiet and passive when a criminal nation invades another nation, taking its freedom away, then God would have to supernaturally intervene by using military angels to provide protection. However, God has established nations that are righteous, and who are willing to intervene in favor of the weaker ones. Again, that is one of the purposes for which God has blessed the United States of America, so this Nation and its allies would be a stronghold for freedom. So, we can see that in this world, there are law-abiding nations and nations that are structured along the frame of criminality. God is a God who stands for righteousness, freedom, and justice, and every nation which goes against that is criminal. Every nation on the face of the earth has the responsibility to establish a Code of Law and to faithfully uphold it as a vital means of survival. When any nation ceases honoring the Code of Law, it is doomed to collapse from within.

King David had transgressed the law of God by numbering the people of Israel. This census was an illegal one, and therefore, in the eyes of the Lord, David had committed a crime and would have to be punished for it. In I Chronicles 21:1, we read,

*"And Satan stood up against Israel, and provoked David to number Israel."* Remember, Satan is the master criminal, and he has established criminality on the earth by influencing people. That is exactly what we see here in this one verse saying "Satan stood up against Israel,

and provoked David..." David committed this crime because he allowed Satan to influence him. That is what criminality is on the earth. That is the reason criminality is addressed here as darkness, and officers of the law stand against this darkness, when on duty.

Now, since there had been a crime committed, and the offense was specifically a violation of God's determinations, and He does not have any tolerance for it, He supernaturally intervened. He sent an avenging angel, and in I Chronicles 21:16 we read,

*"And David lifted up his eyes, and saw the angel of the Lord stand between the earth and the heaven, having a drawn sword in his hand stretched out over Jerusalem. Then David and the elders of Israel, who were clothed in sackcloth, fell upon their faces."*

This one angel would serve in the capacity of a military angel, to reiterate the fact that angels have been used for the sake of law and order when laws are transgressed by nations or individuals. They were active as such, long before humanity organized law enforcement agencies.

To wrongdoers, there is nothing more terrifying than an angel standing there with a sword in his hand. All officers of the law project that same image in the realm of the natural. People must be reminded of what law enforcement personnel represents. They are sworn in to uphold the law. Lawmakers write laws, and when approved, these laws become the will of the people. The government represents the people and has the authority to use all of its power to maintain law and order. The criminal positions himself against that power and authority and stands in direct opposition to the law. The criminal is an enemy of the people and must not prevail. I want to remind people again that criminality is war declared against society. This is not being too harsh, too conservative, or too radical, it is only a fact.

In the Book of Joshua 5:13-15, we have Joshua's account of his encounter with an angel as follows:

*"And it came to pass, when Joshua was by Jericho, that he lifted his eyes and looked, and behold, a Man stood opposite him with His sword drawn in His hand. And Joshua went to Him and said to Him, Are You for us or for our adversaries? So He said, No, but as Commander of the army of the Lord I have now come. And Joshua fell on his face to the earth and worshiped, and said to Him, what does my Lord say to His servant? Then the Commander of the Lord's army said to Joshua, take your sandal off your foot, for the place where you stand is holy. And Joshua did so."*

Angels have ranks, and this one was a commander and a ranked officer. This text is an indication that on planet earth, there is always a battle between good and evil. This struggle is the direct result of the crime committed by Lucifer, even as recorded in the Book of Isaiah 14:12-15, and in the Book of Ezekiel 28:15-19, as noted previously. The archetype of criminality has been active, attempting to influence individuals, cities, states, and nations. He continues to persist in his rebellion against God and has been active in the belief that every human being he can influence, adds to his strength, and represents a defeat to God.

Remember, Jesus Christ came to die on the cross for the entire humanity, which is the heart of God, and therefore, Lucifer believes that each person he moves away from God's saving power represents a blow to God's saving plan and sovereignty. Lucifer, as a criminal, is very disruptive, and God's saving plan is a matter of law and order in the universe, and he stands against it. That is the reason I keep saying that there is more to criminality than we see happening on earth. Criminality is a problem, a real problem within the physical and the metaphysical realms.

The paramilitary and military angels do provide protection, and they assist people in battles. It is possible that the angels of God helped the American soldiers when America entered the First and Second World Wars because they represented that which is good on the earth, as a Nation. No, I am not saying that America is a perfect nation, but that as a nation, America is willing to go to war to set captive people free. And that is a powerful principle in this universe of God.

According to the historical account of the Bible, angels have operated as evacuators as happened in Sodom and Gomorrah. In this particular situation, angels performed the duties that law enforcement personnel perform nowadays, in the case of earthquakes, hurricanes, and other major natural disasters. In the Book of Genesis 19:1, we have the arrival of the two angels. These two angels had been with Abraham in Genesis 18:1-16. The third angel, referred to as the "Lord" in Genesis 18:2, had stayed behind, and Abraham pleaded with him for the preservation of Sodom and Gomorrah, as recorded in Genesis 18:23-33, where we read,

*"And Abraham came near and said, "Would You also destroy the righteous with the wicked? Suppose there were fifty righteous within the city; would You also destroy the place and not spare it for the fifty righteous that were in it? Far be it from You to do such a thing as this, to slay the righteous with the wicked, so that the righteous should be as the wicked; far be it from You! Shall not the Judge of all the earth do right?" So the Lord said, "If I find in Sodom fifty righteous within the city, then I will spare all the place for their sakes." Then Abraham answered and said, "Indeed now, I who am but dust and ashes have taken it upon myself to speak to*

*the Lord: Suppose there were five less than the fifty righteous; would You destroy all of the city for lack of five?" So He said, "If I find there forty-five, I will not destroy it." And he spoke to Him yet again and said, "Suppose there should be forty found there?" So He said, "I will not do it for the sake of forty." Then he said, "Let not the Lord be angry, and I will speak: Suppose thirty should be found there?" So He said, "I will not do it if I find thirty there." And he said, "Indeed now, I have taken it upon myself to speak to the Lord: Suppose twenty should be found there?"*

*So He said, "I will not destroy it for the sake of twenty." Then he said, "Let not the Lord be angry, and I will speak but once more: Suppose ten should be found there?" And He said, "I will not destroy it for the sake of ten." So the Lord went His way as soon as He had finished speaking with Abraham; and Abraham returned to his place."*

This one angel was an appearance of the pre-incarnate Christ. The two angels that went into Sodom are known in the Bible as walkers or watchers and appear to have no wings, but as angelical beings, they could move with the speed of thought if needed. They thought about being somewhere and simultaneously, they were there. They ate food, drank water, slept, and rested. In Genesis 19:1 we read, "Now the two angels came to Sodom in the evening, and Lot was sitting in the gate of Sodom." These angels are always focused on the task ahead, and in Genesis 19:15-17 we have the description of their reason for coming to these cities, which was as follows:

*"When the morning dawned, the angels urged Lot to hurry, saying, "Arise, take your wife and your two daughters who are here, lest you be consumed in the punishment of the city." And while he lingered, the men took hold of his hand, his wife's hand, and the hands of his two daughters, the Lord being merciful to him, and they brought him out and set him outside the city. So it came to pass, when they had brought them outside, that he said "Escape for your life! Do not look behind you nor stay anywhere in the plain. Escape to the mountains, lest you be destroyed."*

It appears that Lot was dragging his feet, and the two angels, well aware of the imminent destruction of the cities, kept rushing him and his family to get out of there. They even grabbed their hands, leading them outside, and then giving them instructions on where to go to be safe. The similarity between the actions of these angels and that of law enforcement, as we know it, when having to evacuate an area in which human lives are at risk, is simply amazing.

So, once more, we can see that angels have performed the same duties law enforcement personnel perform in modern societies. The duties of these angels include fighting criminality in the universe, and even here on earth as done in times past.

The problem originates from the moment Lucifer broke the law in Heaven, by becoming rebellious and attempting to take over God's Throne. We have seen how Lucifer refused to leave Heaven, and his refusal led to a war in Heaven in which the angels of God fought against Lucifer and his angels, but the angels of God prevailed, and Lucifer and his angels were cast down to the earth. We have a record of that incident in Revelation 12:7-9 where we read,

*"And war broke out in heaven: Michael and his angels fought with the dragon; and the dragon and his angels fought, but they did not prevail, nor was a place found for them in heaven any longer. So, the great dragon was cast out, that serpent of old, called the Devil and Satan, who deceives the whole world; he was cast to the earth, and his angels were cast out with him."*

Our focus has been set on the fact that angels are the real role models for all law enforcement personnel, and not just here in the United States of America, but in every nation on the face of the earth which are indeed nations of laws. Without laws a nation becomes profane; it still has sovereignty, but its sovereignty could become a harbor for the criminal head of state. Without laws, the authority given by God becomes an instrument of injustice and oppression. The Code of Law is sacred, and it needs to be revered, and enforcing the Code of Law is the primary responsibility of all legally established governments. God has had, in times past, angels enforcing the laws, and that is evidence to us that criminality must not prevail and that all those criminals who represent a threat to society, must be removed and isolated from other people until they learn how to live in harmony with the rest of society.

This removal of the criminal angels was done in Heaven and must also be done on earth where criminal individuals must also be removed from society. Ezekiel 28:17 states:

*"And you sinned; Therefore, I cast you as a profane thing out of the mountain of God; And I destroyed you, O covering cherub, from the midst of the fiery stones."*

Here we see that the archetype of criminality was removed from the mountain of God, and also *"from the midst of the fiery stones,"* which were other angels in Heaven. This action is a necessity, and to keep criminals mixed with the rest of the population is to provide them with the opportunity to commit other crimes. If a legally established government decides that its laws are too harsh and unfair to criminals and that they will give them a chance to be out of county jails and out of prisons, believing that this is better justice, they certainly can, for they have the authority to do so. If this same government desires to ignore the example given by God on how to deal with criminality, they also can do that. If the government wants to keep law enforcement personnel from getting too involved with criminality, they certainly can. Any level of human authority that desires to be a bit more affable toward criminals can do that, but as a rule, criminals will take advantage of the situation, and instead of improving themselves, they will get worse. This initiative of being progressive and becoming more tolerant toward criminality is definitely an error of judgment, and allow me to say, it is a disfavor to criminals who could be led to rethink their lifestyle by experiencing the restraining power of the legal system.

## Military Activity in Heaven

That's right! That is exactly what Ezekiel describes in his vision. In the Book of Ezekiel 1:7, we read:

*"Their legs were straight, and the soles of their feet were like the soles of calves' feet. They sparkled like the color of burnished bronze."*

Notice that their legs are straight indicating they are in a military type of activity.

In verse 9 we read: *"Their wings touched one another. The creatures did not turn when they went, but each one went straight forward."* This verse 9 gives us a more complete description of their behavior. The wings touching one another indicates a perfect formation, and that of an army force marching down a street or road.

In verse 12 we read, *"And each one went straight forward; they went wherever the spirit wanted them to go, and they did not turn when they went."*

What we have in these three verses, is the description of a military drill, in Heaven. Notice that they went straight forward, and did not turn sideways, and that is the behavior of an army when marching. But let's take a look at verse 24 where we read:

*"When they went, I heard the noise of their wings, like the noise of many waters, like the voice of the Almighty, a tumult like the noise of an army;"* NKJV says *"a tumult like the noise of an army."* New Life Version states: *"They sounded like the noise of an army camp."*

The Wycliffe Bible:

*"... and like the sound of armies in battle;"*

What is going on? Heaven was on high alert! Why? Because there was a criminal on the loose, and he was refusing to leave Heaven, which is going to lead to a war in Heaven, according to the vision of John, in Revelation 12:7-9, where we read:

*"And war broke out in heaven: Michael and his angels fought with the dragon; and the dragon and his angels fought, but they did not prevail, nor was a place found for them in heaven any longer. So, the great dragon was cast out, that serpent of old, called the Devil and Satan, who deceives the whole world; he was cast to the earth, and his angels were cast out with him."*

All this should help us realize how serious criminality is. The reality of criminality has placed the entire universe at risk, and it also causes human civilization to be at risk.

I don't believe that we are even able to fully grasp the real impact of criminality upon the entire universe. The most genius of human beings would still be too naïve to have such an insight, especially into the unseen realm of the universe. Besides being naïve, we are also trapped inside our physical senses, so we become unable to properly evaluate that which is beyond our physicality. We are too small, too insignificant to have a real grasp of our beginnings, and coming into it at the tail end of things, causes us to miss a lot, and the only source of information that we have regarding that side of our history is the Bible, that many people reject as being a collection of fables. No, we are already extremely limited in that which we know, and by rejecting divine information, we put ourselves in a bubble, and create a condition in which we are trying to handle our affairs under the false assumption that we are in control. And when it comes to false assumptions, we are at our best!

Truth is, that, in a universe in which all creatures live in peace and harmony with each other, and one in which all created beings live in total submission to the Creator, there would be no need for the presence of military power. But when a crime has been committed, and all criminality is, to one degree or another, a form of rebellion against the established authority, then a wall of defense has to be raised for the protection of people and the environment. That happened first in Heaven when Lucifer decided that he wanted to be the ruler of the universe.

Angels with swords, as described in the Old Testament, can be perceived as strange and even dramatic, especially to those people who have no insight into their own spirituality and that of the universe. It has become so much easier to ignore the teachings of the Bible, than to try to figure it out, bringing people to another aspect of their false assumptions, which is if they don't see or hear it, it does not exist.

So, in Ezekiel 1: 7, 9, and 12, we have angels appearing to be in a military type of activity in a stunning scenario in Heaven. Military activities in Heaven; who would have imagined? In Genesis 3:24, we have the Cherubims guarding the entrance of the Garden, with the presence of a flaming sword at their reach. In I Chronicles 21:16, King David watched an angel standing between heaven and earth, having a drawn sword in his hand. In Joshua 5:13, Joshua in the vicinity of Jericho lifted his eyes and saw an angel with a drawn sword in his hand. The carrying of swords is one of the most important aspects of them being considered to be military and paramilitary angels. They did not carry a sword as a piece of decoration. We all know that a sword is a weapon of defense and also offense. There would be absolutely no need for the presence of swords in the entire universe if no peril existed. Symbolically, even the word of God is considered to be a sword, as described in Hebrews 4:12, where we read:

*"For the word of God is living and powerful, and sharper than any two-edged sword, piercing even to the division of soul and spirit, and of joints and marrow, and is a discerner of the thoughts and intents of the heart."*
And also, in Ephesians 6:17, we read:

*"And take the helmet of salvation, and the sword of the Spirit, which is the word of God;"*

The word of God, depicted as a sword, is based on the reality of the universe, which is filled with both physical and metaphysical dangers.

When we consider all the perils existent in our environment, then police work becomes the most essential work to be done.

The established authorities do have the responsibility to protect every person under their influence, but criminals do not fit into that category. Criminals do have one right, which is the right to a fair and just legal process in court.

## Principality and Powers of Criminality

Angels have a hierarchy as we read in Daniel 10:21, and also in 12: 1, where Michael is referred to as a "Prince." Michael is an archangel, and the biblical text tells us of three archangels: Michael, Gabriel, and Lucifer, or Satan. These are chief angels, and we are given the idea that these three angels were in charge of all other angels. Each had a third of the angels under him. The reason for this rationale is found in Revelation 12:4, where we read:

*"His tail drew a third of the stars of heaven:"*

This is a reference to the fallen angel, Lucifer, and the third of the stars he dragged down with him refers to those angels that were under his authority. He was and still is a prince, although he has forfeited his place in Heaven with the other angels that remain faithful to God. We see in another biblical instance that Michael acknowledges Lucifer as a prince by avoiding passing judgment on him, even as we read in Jude 9, saying:

*"Yet Michael the archangel, in contending with the devil, when he disputed about the body of Moses, dared not bringing against him a reviling accusation, but said 'The Lord rebuke you!'"*

People may wonder why God did not annihilate this one angel. The answer is for the same reason he has not annihilated the entirety of humanity. Truth is, God does have the power to execute justice and destroy evil-doers, but God would be a criminal himself if, after giving His creatures free will, would destroy them for exercising that same free will. In the case of Lucifer, he was removed from Heaven by God, allowing him and the third of the angels under him to inhabit the realm around the earth, although they can't be physically seen because they have no corporality or physical bodies. But, because they are not seen, does not mean they are not there.

God cannot defeat criminality or evil, by making use of his divine power. God has integrity, and he cannot be moved to act against his determination, and in this case, He gave His creature volitional capability. God cannot do and undo just because He is God. When God gave the earth to mankind, He gave them dominion over everything on earth, and that is stated in Genesis 1:26,

*"And God said, let us make man in our image, after our likeness: and let them have dominion... over all the earth."* Now people do have the option to abide by the principles of God, or not. Remember, there is a criminal on the loose, and he will not miss the chance of asserting his influence on people. We don't have all the facts, but it is possible that without the availability of people, Lucifer would lose his foothold on earth, and therefore would no longer be able to remain in the vicinity of the earth.

The only way evil could come into the universe would have to be through decision-making. Lucifer decided he could win the struggle against God and would remove God from His throne. Lucifer made that determination in his own heart, as stated in Ezekiel 28:15,

*"You were perfect in your ways from the day you were created, till iniquity was found in you."*

Iniquity was found in him, meaning that he thought about, established an intention, then acted upon it, and it all started within him. So, the Prophet Ezekiel tells us that in the heart of Lucifer, we have the source of evil. And we must keep in perspective that evil is the equivalent of criminality.

In Revelation 12:7-9 we have the description of a war fought in Heaven between the angels of God and

Lucifer and his angels. Lucifer and his angels lost that war and were cast down to earth in total defeat. In Ezekiel 28:18, we read,

*"You defiled your sanctuaries by the multitude of your iniquities, By the iniquity of your trading; Therefore, I brought fire from your midst; It devoured you, and I turned you to ashes upon the earth In the sight of all who saw you."*

Notice God said, *"I brought fire from your midst, it devoured you, and I turned you to ashes upon the earth..."* This is evidence that God had not annihilated Lucifer but had spoken a prophetic word toward him rendering him a defeated foe, over time. When Lucifer saw Adam and Eve in the Garden and knew God had given them dominion on earth, he saw his opportunity to re-initiate his opposition to God by establishing a degree of control within people. He would not have had access to the human person, or into human affairs, unless man gave him access, as we read,

*"Now the serpent was more cunning than any beast of the field which the Lord God had made. And he said to the woman, "Has God indeed said, 'You shall not eat of every tree of the garden'?" And the woman said to the serpent, "We may eat the fruit of the trees of the garden; but of the fruit of the tree which is in the midst of the garden, God has said, 'You shall not eat it, nor shall*

*you touch it, lest you die.' Then the serpent said to the woman, "You will not surely die. For God knows that in the day you eat of it your eyes will be opened, and you will be like God, knowing good and evil." So when the woman saw that the tree was good for food, that it was pleasant to the eyes, and a tree desirable to make one wise, she took of its fruit and ate. She also gave to her husband with her, and he ate."* (Genesis 3:1-6).

So, the source of evil and darkness in the entire universe had been found within Lucifer, and now the source of evil and darkness on the entire earth had been established within the human person. According to the text of Genesis 3:1-6, Lucifer had complete success in turning mankind into lawbreakers.

Potentially, every human being is a criminal. In Psalms 51:5 it is stated: *"Behold, I was brought forth iniquity, and in sin my mother conceived me."* The term iniquity means to be *without law, or lawless.* God deals with the lawlessness of man by offering him forgiveness in the Lord Jesus Christ, but man must deal with lawlessness by enforcing the Code of Law. Therefore, both the Code of Law and law enforcement are absolute necessities, here on earth.

Lucifer had been completely neutralized regarding his intention of taking over God's throne. God passed judgment on Lucifer and determined that his final defeat would be brought about on planet earth. In Ezekiel 28:18 we read,

*"You defiled your sanctuaries by the multitude of your iniquities, by the iniquity of your trading; Therefore, I brought fire from your midst; It devoured you, and I turned you to ashes upon the earth."*

He had lost his place in Heaven, but Lucifer had found another way! He decided that if he could intrude into the affairs of mankind, then he could become again a foe to be reckoned with. And that is the reason why Saint Paul said:

*"For we wrestle not against flesh and blood, but against principalities, and powers, against the rulers of the darkness of this world, against spiritual wickedness (lawlessness) in high places."* (Ephesians 6:12).

That is the resistance that the people of faith go against every day, and that is the problem law enforcement personnel deal with daily. The use of the words *"principalities and powers,"* is an indication to us that unless we use the correct source of power to deal with it, we might lose the fight. We have two ways by which we can defeat evil, one is by relying on the sacrificial death of the Lord Jesus Christ for the salvation of each believer, and the other is to fight evil by enforcing the Code of Law.

The spirit of evil or criminality can only be stopped by proper authority. In the case of the human person's sinfulness, it is the authority established by the Lord Jesus Christ's death on Calvary. Evil or criminality, as in the transgression of the laws of man, must be defeated by the use of the authority of the law. And that is the authority that all law enforcement personnel represent. Anyone taking the initiative to disempower law enforcement is only giving chaos a chance.

Lucifer, the archetype of criminality, has the freedom to move on the face of the earth as he pleases. This is an understanding we get from Ephesians 6:12, and also from the Book of Job 1:6-7, where we read,

*"Now there was a day when the sons of God came to present themselves before the Lord, and Satan also came among them. And the Lord said to Satan, "From where do you come?" So Satan answered the Lord and said, "From going to and fro on the earth, and from walking back and forth on it."* Lucifer and his fallen angels do not have corporality and therefore have no legal right to operate on the earth. They are intruders, and that is the reason they are referred to as alien entities. The reason he is still hanging around is that in the Garden of Eden, Adam and Eve fell for his trick, and people continue to

give him a foothold which is exactly what Saint Paul advised people not to do, saying:

*"nor give* place *to the devil." (Ephesians 4:27).*

He lost his place in Heaven, but he has been persistent here on earth, and men and women who continuously break the laws of society, have given him a place in their minds. They are not possessed by the devil, they are only thinking as he thinks, in the same way that the law-abiding person is also thinking as God thinks. These two elements are opposing elements on the earth. Only the law-abiding person must prevail, the other one must reconsider or pay the price required by the law.

The human mind is the battleground! Criminality, when chronic, becomes a mindset and an attitude. The individual who has developed an attitude of criminality is pretty much consumed by it. That is all he knows, and his thoughts and intentions are generally always turned in the direction of committing a crime.

In the Book of Proverbs 23:7, we read: *"As he thinks in his heart, so is he;"*

The thought pattern of criminals is shaped by the disposition to be lawless. The greatest part of people living on this earth understand that it is in their best interest to be lawful. They do not have any difficulty in arriving at this conclusion, and they have made themselves profitable to society, to themselves, and to their families, and they have no problem living their lives this way. A great number of these people are not necessarily what one would call Godly, and they may not even be religious at all, but they know enough to desire to live their lives within the boundaries of the law.

Only the law-abiding person can serve humanity, and at a minimal level, they serve humanity by having an understanding of the importance of cooperating for the peace of mind of the community. These ones have learned the importance of having respect for other people and their belongings. The law-abiding person has a good attitude, is easy to get along with, and they are an asset to society.

The criminal does not know how to live in society. He is disruptive, and he generates fear and insecurity in other people. He, for as long as he persists in living his life against the law, is unable to recognize mercy and compassion. He is going in the wrong direction and needs the help of the law to be turned around. Notice, I said he needs the help of the law if he is to be turned from his criminal ways. The laws of men are based on right and wrong, black and white, and if flexibility is allowed, it needs to be a provision of the law itself. The legal system is sovereign, and it cannot be treated with contempt. When a person appears before a judge in any court of law, this person must be very careful what he says, in fact, here in America, one needs to be careful with what he says even during an arrest. Why? When an individual is before the law, whether he is dealing with law enforcement or in the presence of a judge, he needs to have the proper respect and reverence, and some people could benefit from being in awe.

Nowadays there is disrespect being generated toward law enforcement, even by some officials who have been elected by the people to serve this nation. If a government official has a problem with how the law is being enforced, he/she needs to have a more effective way to deal with it rather than negative criticism verbalized in public. This lack of reverence for law enforcement, on the part of people in leadership, has caused individuals to call for the death of police officers during public manifestations, and a great segment of people in government remain silent about it. Why? Because they probably felt that those death threats toward police officers, better serve their political ideology. This is a nation of laws, and it must continue to be so, and that kind of behavior is absolutely unacceptable. People in a position of authority, elected by the people to serve, should not be promoting lawlessness. No, not here in America!

Criminality is a threat to society, and law enforcement represents the authority of the entire society. When a segment of the population is being turned against police officers to the point where they are now a target of the misfit and irreverent, and this is being condoned by people in authority, it is shameful and unacceptable! It is evident that the archetype of criminality has been busy, and he is now committing one of his favorite crimes, which is to create division so that One Nation under God, no longer exists as such. That is what he does best; he works in the minds of people, in the way they think, and in that way, he establishes his principality and power. He loves influencing people holding positions of authority, and after that, he rules by influencing their thoughts and their intentions. Lucifer is a master in the formation of mental strongholds. That is what he does in the lives of people before he turns them into criminals. Yes, he can be a prince again, and he can have power again, but only in the lives of people who allow him to manipulate their minds.

Criminals can only respond to their crimes in two places within the universe: in Heaven or on earth. If two people go to Mars, and once there, one kills the other, the murderer can only be judged by the courts here on earth. There is no court system established on Mars. But even if we had a court system on Mars, it would have to be established by humans, because humans alone have been given authority and dominion on earth. Therefore, a human criminal can only be held responsible before people and before God.

Criminality has affected the state of heavenly beings and has also completely altered the reality of earthly beings. Being tough on crime should not be a matter of being liberal or conservative, but because it is the best approach to combat it. Either we control criminality, or it will control us. And that is what police officers do best. They control criminality by enforcing laws written by elected lawmakers. And when lawmakers become soft on crime, people in society find themselves trying to live life within a disrupted environment. When duly elected officials start tampering with law enforcement, families find themselves not having protection and with increased vulnerability to the elements of criminality within the community. So, the cover of proper authority over the people has been replaced, the presence of disruptive individuals has increased, and we'll have Lucifer establishing his principality and power over society, and life will have become darker. Injustice and unfairness for all are taking place. And what else is going on? The most common crime committed by elected officials is the crime of neglecting the people's needs. Remember, law enforcement is a necessity, not a privilege!

Now, concerning criminals being held responsible before God in Heaven, we have Daniel describing a vision he had, saying:

*"I watched till thrones were put in place, And the Ancient of Days was seated; His garment was white as*

*snow, and the hair of His head was like pure wool. His throne was a fiery flame, its wheels a burning fire; a fiery stream issued and came forth from before Him. A thousand, thousand ministered to Him; ten thousand times ten thousand stood before Him. The court was seated, and the books were opened."* (Daniel 7:9-10).

God's judgment is imminent. People can make peace with him now, by complying with the words of Saint John 3:18, saying:

*"He that believes on him is not condemned: but he that believes not is condemned already, because he has not believed in the name of the only begotten Son of God."*

So, everybody has a choice of making peace with God now, as we read in Romans 5:1,

*"Therefore, being justified by faith, we have peace with God through our Lord Jesus Christ:"*

So, God is willing to give every criminal the opportunity, right now, to become oriented according to His righteousness, and Saint Paul states:

*"For he has made him to be sin for us, who knew no sin; that we might be made the righteousness of God in him."* (II Corinthians 5:21).

God has given every human being, the opportunity to be declared righteous, by placing their faith in the Lord Jesus Christ, and if they refuse to benefit by internalizing the divine offer, then they have been scheduled to appear before God, the Eternal Judge, as described in the vision of Daniel 7:9-10 saying:

> "I watched till thrones were put in place, And the Ancient of Days was seated;
> His garment was white as snow, And the hair of His head was like pure wool.
> His throne was a fiery flame, Its wheels a burning fire; A fiery stream issued
> And came forth from before Him. A thousand, thousand ministered to Him;
> Ten thousand times ten thousand stood before Him. The court was seated,
> And the books were opened."

Picture it yourself, that entire humanity has been thrown inside of a funnel, and upon coming out at the bottom of the funnel, we have God waiting, and no one can escape it. Saint John also tells us what condemnation is, stating: *"And this is the condemnation, that light is come into the world, and men loved darkness rather than light, because their deeds were evil."* (John 3:19).

Criminality is darkness, and criminals have to be held accountable before God and before men. We must be governed by the principles of the word of God, and we must make a conscious decision to adopt the Code of Law as the pathway to a life of peace and quietness.

## Resist the Criminal

To resist the archetype of criminality is an advisement of the word of God. Saint Peter said:

*"Be sober, be vigilant; because your adversary the devil, as a roaring lion, walks about, seeking whom he may devour: whom resist steadfast in the faith, knowing that the same afflictions are accomplished in your brethren that are in the world."* (I Peter 5:8-9).

Here, the Apostle is speaking to believers, but he is also directing his words toward humanity. The reason is that Lucifer unleashed an attack on the entire human race when he succeeded in getting Adam and Eve to say yes to his propositions. Sure, he is busy attacking those who are of the faith but do not overlook the fact that he is also busy attacking humanity. That is why we have the problem of criminality, and at times it appears to be getting completely out of hand. He attacks humanity from top to bottom. What does that mean? He has penetrated the sphere of government, intending to turn the heads of nations, such as kings, military generals, prime ministers, and presidents, into criminals. That is the reason Saint Paul wrote:

*"Exhort therefore, that, first of all, supplications, prayers, intercessions, and giving of thanks, be made for all men; for kings, and for all that are in authority; that*

*we may lead a quiet and peaceful life in all godliness and honesty. For this is good and acceptable in the sight of God our Savior."* I Timothy 2:1-3).

So, the Apostle requests prayers in favor of kings and people in authority. Why? Because Lucifer likes to attack the head, and the head of every nation is its government. He turns them into criminals, causing the oppression of the people. Lucifer enjoys enslaving people, and he is not particular about the color of their skin. The Prophet Isaiah said this about Lucifer,

*"That made the world as a wilderness, and destroyed the cities thereof; that opened not the house of his prisoners"* (Isaiah 14:17)?

Lucifer brings people into his prison, and he is never willing to open the door so they can walk out. He is merciless and has no compassion. He turns them into criminals, and if they do not seek help from the Lord, and if the laws of men let them fall through the cracks, then there is no help for them. The master criminal is never willing to help because he is always focused on the worsening of people's mental and spiritual condition.

Lucifer wants the Code of Law to be softened, and nowadays we have plenty of rulers who are willing to do so, in the name of compassion and justice. There is a notion that there has been enough injustice committed toward criminals and that in the modern world, we have to do better. Some believe that human beings cannot be treated unfairly and that we must be humane. But the truth is that criminals do have a choice: to not live as transgressors of the law. They need to be willing to change their ways, to create better lives for themselves. But this has to be the result of their own initiative, to be valid.

In a world controlled by liberals/socialists, the criminals do get plenty of breaks, not because these liberals/socialists care about the welfare of people, but rather because they hate a conservative world.

So, this offer to help, and disposition to be merciful and compassionate, is actually enablement to commit more crimes. These people have an agenda, and it is not the agenda of the people. We should be taking away from people the space to commit a crime, instead of opening even more channels for them to do so. That is what enablement does! It has the appearance of assistance, but in reality, it is extremely harmful. Enablement is the behavior of co-dependent people. And government systems have been infiltrated by those who are co-dependent with wrongdoers. What is worst of all, is that they have to kick the behind of law enforcement personnel to do so.

To side with wrongdoers, you must not be doing a good job resisting Lucifer. If there is any police officer who is not being resistant to Lucifer, they will look the other way while a crime is being committed. In this case, the police officer is not fit for the job! His neglect toward the commission of a crime is, in itself, a moral crime. This police officer is no longer for the people but against the people. The same could be said of those in a higher level of authority, whenever they decide that embracing criminals is a better way to do their jobs.

Lucifer favors criminality because that is him at his best. He wants law enforcement to be attacked, and to be demoralized. In fact, I think he is behind that effort, all the way. Because with crime comes darkness, and darkness is his favorite realm. Saint Paul says that God loves to bring people out of the darkness, saying,

*"Who has delivered us from the power of darkness, and has translated us into the kingdom of his dear Son"* (Colossians 1:13).

But Lucifer's primary task is to bring people out of the light, and into his darkness. Police officers are not using the Bible to enforce the law, but making use of the Code of Law is how they fight against darkness every time they are on duty. They are not in church houses, but out in the streets, constantly risking their own lives.

When an individual breaks the law, and a police officer, by listening to his story, finds out he has had a tough life and cuts him loose, the officer is being neglectful. If the criminal goes before a judge, and the judge, upon hearing his story, also determines that he has had a history of traumatic events in his life and cuts him some slack, the judge is being negligent, and both the judge and police officer are being enablers. Their attempt to help is not really helping. People who have suffered prejudices and discrimination, and who may have grown up in poverty, should not be the reason for the entire justice system to change. A whole lot of people have been discriminated against throughout the entire face of the earth; is that reason enough to give them a break if they transgress the law? Let me repeat this: people have a better choice in life, and that is to obey the law. People might not have had a choice about being born into poverty or being born white, black, yellow, or red, but they most definitely have a choice in how they live their lives! Do not allow Lucifer to take you down to a life of criminality. Resist him! People can resist him spiritually by making use of their faith, just as Saint Peter suggested, or they can resist him morally. Both of these ways are the possibility that mankind has.

The truth is that whether a person lives his life by the standards of the word of God or not, criminality should never be an option. People who do not consider themselves to be spiritual still have a moral obligation to be law-abiding. This is a requirement if we want to live in society. People who have chosen to not follow the steps of the Lord Jesus Christ and to not implement his teachings in their lives are still expected to honor the Code of Law and to respect law enforcement personnel also.

# The Criminal Head of State

In Romans 13:1, Saint Paul very clearly states that there is no authority in this entire universe unless it is that which comes from God. This is a tremendous statement because human beings are accustomed to thinking that they are in control and that they are the source of their power. God must always remind mankind that He is the source of everything that can be observed in this universe. The authority to govern means to have power over others. Power is extremely corrupting, and most people are not prepared for such power. There are two elements that God has given mankind that are usually misused by most: riches and power. To many who are confused in their way of thinking, riches, and power are the same. From God's perspective, and according to His purpose, riches, and power are elements to help human beings live in an environment of freedom, justice, and fairness. When heads of state use their position of power and influence to enrich themselves, they become criminals themselves. They are no longer using divine authority under the direction of God, but they have become corrupted by allowing the archetype of criminality to influence them. And, just like Lucifer, when the criminal is in power, he will kill, steal and destroy (John 10:10).

People tend to perceive the criminal head of state as being insane. No, he is not insane, he is just influenced by Lucifer himself, and that is the reason they strike others as being insane. Insanity is a mental illness, and no mentally ill person can be that functional. The perception of most human beings, when someone does something completely out of the norm, is to label that person crazy. They say, "He is crazy," or "She is crazy!" In reality, the person is not crazy; he/she is only going against the norm. To most people, I mean, to people who are law-abiding citizens, to rob a bank is crazy, or it is insane, some would say. But truthfully, the bank robber is not crazy or insane, he is just thinking like a criminal.

When a head of state invades another country, is he being crazy and insane, or is he acting like he has Lucifer's mind? He is only acting according to the power which influences him. No head of state who has been influenced by God has ever invaded another country to enslave and kill people. That is not the purpose of divinely-given authority, and that is not what divine influence leads to. So, we have two sources of power in the universe, both very active, and both target the human mind.

God represents light and life, and Lucifer represents darkness and death. God is for people to be law-abiding, and Lucifer wants people to be lawless. It is that simple! That is why the United States can be considered to be a good nation, not perfect, but good because, from the very beginning, the forefathers planned a nation that would be established on divine principles. Why would anyone in America argue against that historic fact? Unless it is because they want to control it themselves. They may have developed the idea that they are that powerful, and they want to run things as they see fit. But I rather have God in control, than men. Well, I would have to be crazy to think otherwise. But no, I am not crazy, I just happen to be the kind of person that would rather be under divine influence than under that of men and/or Lucifer.

I know what men are capable of doing when they are not under the influence of God. They have the potential to become criminals, and when in a position of power and authority, individuals become the target of Lucifer. He likes turning governments into tyrannical systems, and tyrannical systems' first initiative is to always cause people the loss of their freedom. In that case, criminality begins when people lose their freedom.

Let people not think that they are not criminals because they don't rob banks and kill people. Leaders of nations become criminals by turning into oppressors of the people. King David shared in the records of the Bible, what the Lord told him about what righteous government really is,

*"The Spirit of the Lord spoke by me, And His word was on my tongue. The God of Israel said, the Rock of Israel spoke to me: 'He who rules over men must be just, ruling in the fear of God. And he shall be like the light of the morning when the sun rises, a morning without clouds, Like the tender grass springing out of the earth, By clear shining after rain"* (II Samuel 23:2-4).

Notice that he says, "He who rules over men must be just, ruling in the fear of God." To God, the idea of having authority requires the presence of justice and fairness for all law-abiding people. To obey the law is the minimum requirement to live in society.

No, the United States is not a criminal nation, and, thanks to its forefathers, the United States of America knows a lot about fairness and justice for all. Above and beyond all, this has been a nation of laws, but I fear that there is a growing movement to convince people that the old and traditional America has been a harmful one and that it needs to be dismantled and rebuilt as a better America for the globe. This nation of ours is under attack, and this attack has been unleashed from within. If the America established on the principles of the word of God is bad, how can we expect America to be better when built on the principles of men? No, the nation cannot be improved that way, but delusional people think that they can get it done. If it ever comes to pass, it is going to be an America without God. Imagine that! And, if a nation is not influenced by God, it is influenced by whom? Just remember this, if you turn off the light, you get darkness. If you "water down" the Code of Law, you only get more transgression of the law. As this movement within America develops and grows stronger, we will see a transition taking place, in which a God-influenced America goes out, and the man-influenced America comes in. But God will have to move aside and give men enough room to establish what they want. And the question is, will God move out of the way?

God raised America to fulfill specific purposes, one of which is to be the principal ally of Israel. The Roman Empire had an eagle, then German Nazis had an eagle, but then came America, and it also has an eagle which is not a common eagle, and I believe that mention is made of America, as the big eagle, in the Book of Revelation. In 12:13-14, we read,

"Now when *the dragon saw that he had been cast to the earth, he persecuted the woman who gave birth to the male Child. But the woman was given <u>two wings of a great eagle,</u> that she might fly into the wilderness to her place, where she is nourished for a time and times and half a time, from the presence of the serpent."*

The woman is Israel, and this text describes a situation that has been unleashed throughout the centuries and will have its final episode in the future when a coalition of nations will gather together under Lucifer's influence and will attempt to annihilate Israel. This coalition of nations will be completely anti-God and anti-Bible.

The United States has been a supporter of Israel beginning in 1947 when President Truman voted in favor of Israel becoming a nation. The United States has remained faithful to that calling of God and will continue to do so, despite some influential people trying to get the US to abandon Israel. The United States will remain the strongest nation on earth, and a strong supporter of Israel for as long as God wants it to, and there is nothing anyone within or without the United States can do to change that. Remember, God reigns and in the Book of Daniel we read,

*"And at the end of the time I, Nebuchadnezzar, lifted my eyes to heaven, and my understanding returned to me; and I blessed the Most-High and praised and honored Him who lives forever: For His dominion is an everlasting dominion, and His kingdom is from generation to generation. All the inhabitants of the earth are reputed as nothing; He does according to His will in the army of heaven and among the inhabitants of the earth. No one can restrain His hand or say to Him, "What have You done?"* (Daniel 4:34-35).

Many nations throughout history attempted to live outside the influence of God and the Code of Law. Some of these nations have disappeared, and some are still around. However, I can say that these nations have done very little toward the improvement of human conditions in the world. Most of these nations are plagued by poverty and are places where people live under oppression. Many of these nations have received outside help from the United States, and from some of the European nations, but the real problem is that these nations are not structured correctly. They don't have a Code of Law that could pass the test of integrity, and many times, the help received from other nations never gets into the hands of the people, where the need lies. So, when the heads of state receive help from other nations aimed at helping the population, but the help received is never equally and fairly divided, then that means that we have criminals in charge. These criminals are hiding behind the "so-called" national sovereignty. Their crime is found in the fact that they are corrupt and oppressive, and they are negligent toward the people they are supposed to be serving.

This is not a new problem around the globe. This has been going on since the very beginning of nations' existence (see Genesis 10). Lucifer saw an opportunity to rule the earth, and he knew that if he established an influence inside the brain of each nation, and its government, he could keep the people of that nation oppressed. He is the real user and the abuser of humanity.

Consider the nation of Egypt, which kept the nation of Israel enslaved for 400 years, (see Exodus 1-13). No consideration for human life, and all that was supposed to be for the benefit of the nation of Egypt. Having an entire nation of people making bricks out of mud, and for what? Let's take a look at the explanation of Pharaoh, saying,

*"Now there arose a new king over Egypt, who did not know Joseph. And he said to his people, "Look, the people of the children of Israel are more and mightier than we; come, let us deal shrewdly with them, lest they multiply, and it happen, in the event of war, that they also join our enemies and fight against us, and so go up out of the land." Therefore, they set taskmasters over them to afflict them with their burdens. And they built for Pharaoh supply cities, Pithom and Raamses."* (Exodus 1:8-11).

That is the rationale of a head of state who does not know God, and who is influenced by the archetype of criminality. Now, a people will live under the strong and cruel hands of taskmasters, which will consistently afflict and oppress them. That is not an authority according to God. This pharaoh is a criminal, and his mind has been influenced by wickedness. The worst thing about a criminal head of state is that he is out of the reach of any law enforcement agency because he hides behind the sovereignty of that nation. It would take the military power of a law-abiding nation, one which believes in freedom, justice, and fairness for all, to go there and set those people free. But, at that time when Israel was being kept in slavery, God had no other nation which He could use, so He had to wait for the right time, and then raise the right person; in this case, Moses was chosen, to set them free.

After Egypt, the other world power was the nation of Babylon. God referred to the king of Babylon as being an oppressor, as we read,

"… .*that you will take up this proverb against the king of Babylon, and say: "How the oppressor has ceased, the golden$_j$ city ceased! The Lord has broken the staff of the wicked, the scepter of the rulers; he who struck the people in wrath with a continual stroke, he who ruled the nations in anger, is persecuted and no one hinders. The whole earth is at rest and quiet; they break forth into singing."* (Isaiah 14:4-7).

Notice verse 7, where we see the earth in a state of quietness and rest, and rejoicing because this criminal ruler is cut down. No, God is not sleeping, neither is He looking the other way, as described by the psalmist, "*Why do the nations rage, and the people plot a vain*

*thing? The kings of the earth set themselves, and the rul-
ers take counsel together, against the Lord and against
His Anointed, saying, "Let us break their bonds in pieces
and cast away their cords from us. "He who sits in the
heavens shall laugh; the Lord shall hold them in derision." (Psalm 2:1-4).*

Tell me, who or what would be behind this con-
temptuous attitude toward God, and His Christ? What
power would cause nations to come together against God
and, to actually think that they can keep God out of their
affairs? It is the work of lawlessness, as always manifested when Lucifer is given room to work. We see this
lawlessness of the nations starting to escalate to more
intense levels, even right now.

Lucifer has always had the opportunity given to
him so he could become the power behind the throne,
in many nations of the earth, in times past. In Babylon,
when Nebuchadnezzar was king, he built a statue of gold
and required everyone in his domain to worship the statue, and whoever refused would be killed. In Daniel 3:4-
6, we read,

*"Then a herald cried aloud: "To you it is command-
ed, O peoples, nations, and languages, that at the time you
hear the sound of the horn, flute, harp, lyre, and psaltery,
in symphony with all kinds of music, you shall fall down
and worship the gold image that King Nebuchadnezzar*

*has set up; and whoever does not fall down and worship shall be cast immediately into the midst of a burning fiery furnace."*

And we know the story of the three Jewish boys, Hananiah, Mishael, and Azariah who refused to worship the image, and what happened to them. They were placed inside the burning, fiery furnace, and only God would be able to deliver them from death. We can see that Nebuchadnezzar became grandiose, thinking that he was God. Of course, he had been deceived by Lucifer, because the whole world knew, and still knows now that the king was not God. But Lucifer knew that causing him to think that he was God, would cause the king to become oppressive, and larger than life, at least in his own eyes. And truthfully, he became a criminal, because he allowed a criminal to influence him. When you determine the death of people because they don't obey your orders, what does that make you? A murderer, like anyone else who takes the life of people unwarrantedly.

It takes God to give authority, and it takes God to remove authority. He had taught Nebuchadnezzar a lesson for life when he removed him from the center of human attention and had him living with the beasts of the field for seven years, as we read in Daniel 4:31-32,

*"While the word was still in the king's mouth, a voice fell from heaven: "King Nebuchadnezzar, to you*

*it is spoken: the kingdom has departed from you! And they shall drive you from men, and your dwelling shall be with the beasts of the field. They shall make you eat grass like oxen; and seven times shall pass over you, until you know that the Most-High rules in the kingdom of men, and gives it to whomever He chooses."*

So, God established him on his throne, but somewhere along the way Lucifer approached him, and became an influence over how the king conducted the affairs of his kingdom, and, in time, the king became more detached from God. Immediately, one of the results of this satanic influence was the loss of value toward human life. People knew that if they displeased the king in the least, it could cost them their lives.

So, God established the man on his throne, and the man allows the spirit of criminality to turn him into a monster, and God then took the power away from him, so, he became insane and found himself living with the animals out in the open environment. Seven years it lasted, and the king himself tells us what happened,

*"And at the end of the time I, Nebuchadnezzar, lifted my eyes to heaven, and my understanding returned to me; and I blessed the Most-High and praised and honored Him who lives forever: For His dominion is an everlasting dominion, and His kingdom is from generation to generation. All the inhabitants of the earth are reputed*

*as nothing; He does according to His will in the army of heaven and among the inhabitants of the earth. No one can restrain His hand or say to Him, "What have You done?"*

*At the same time, my reason returned to me, and for the glory of my kingdom, my honor and splendor returned to me. My counselors and nobles resorted to me, I was restored to my kingdom, and excellent majesty was added to me. Now I, Nebuchadnezzar, praise and extol and honor the King of heaven, all of whose works are truth, and His ways justice. And those who walk in pride He is able to put down."* (Daniel 4:34-37).

The Book of Daniel ought to be read by all people in authority. Presidents, prime ministers, governors, mayors, chiefs of police, judges, and everyone else holding positions of power. They should read it to learn that God is watching and that although He is remaining silent right now, He is still watching. People in a position of authority and power should be careful not to become arrogant and must be constantly aware that they are not the beginning and the end, the first and the last, and the alpha and omega. Only Jesus Christ is all that, and everyone else besides Jesus must always remember that they are finite, and in many ways, extremely limited in their power.

Nebuchadnezzar learned that God rules in the kingdom of men, and that is a lesson that all rulers must learn. God took a criminal king, a dictator ruling in tyranny and arrogance, with no regard for human life, and made him a law-abiding king, and an example to many who are in power, even today.

The Roman Emperors could have done themselves a favor by being submissive to God, instead of yielding power to Lucifer. Great men became losers because of that. Men, who could have, literally, ruled the world if they had remained faithful to God, but because they allowed the archetype of criminality to guide them, they were swallowed up by shame.

I think of the church leaders and how they turned into monsters, persecuting, incarcerating, torturing, and killing those who no longer agreed with their dogmas. Do you mean to tell me that you torture people, and even kill them by burning them alive in the stakes, to preserve the integrity of the church? The horrors of criminality, and how people always find a way to justify it!

## The War on Earth

Let me briefly line up Satan's plan and purpose:
- Manipulate the human mind, so he can establish an internal locus of control.
- Continue what he started in the Garden of Eden, by convincing people that nobody can be sure

about the meaning of the Word of God, and his argument is to convince people that God is ambiguous, (Genesis 3:1-5).

- Satan knows that the integrity of God is in that which He says, and if he can prove God wrong, even with one word He has said, then Satan would probably win this war.
- He thinks that if he can dethrone God in the lives of people, then to that degree, he is winning the war. In his delusional state, he certainly thinks so.
- Satan knows exactly what God desires for human beings and life on earth, and he is fighting to take the course of humanity in an opposite direction to that which God wants.
- Satan knows God is for law and order, so he must declare himself as being against law and order.
- Satan knows God intends for governments of nations to be fair and just, and so he tries his best to establish a dictatorship in positions of power.
- Satan knows God is for freedom, so he influences governments toward becoming oppressors of the people.
- He knows God is pro-life, so he loves when a leader of a nation has no regard for human life.
- He knows God is for lawful governments, and so he becomes profoundly satisfied when the lawless

are in power. Just look at and consider the history of the nations of the earth, and you can see his influence in all kinds of rulership. When the government of a nation is unlawful, that brings a cloud of darkness over the people of that nation. That means criminality is ruling.

- Satan wants people looting/stealing, and vandalizing. He desires that people become physically, emotionally, and mentally abusive to others. He wants people to commit acts of aggression and violence toward others, and he wants them to kill each other. In Revelation 9:20-21, the Apostle John states that people refused to repent of their criminality, and he makes mention of idolatry, worship of demons, sexual immorality, and murders.

In Ezekiel 28:18, we read:

*"You defiled your sanctuaries by the multitude of your iniquities, By the iniquity of your trading; therefore, I brought fire from your midst; It devoured you, And I turned you to ashes upon the earth in the sight of all who saw you."* In the Book of Revelation, we read *"So the great dragon was cast out, that serpent of old, called the Devil and Satan, who deceives the whole world; he was cast to the earth, and his angels were cast out with him."* Revelation 12:9).

God determined that the earth would be the place where Lucifer was going to be defeated. But we also know now that the fight against darkness and criminality would be continued here on the earth. And how do we fight the darkness? We fight it with the Code of Law being faithfully enforced. The criminal needs the laws of the land to be enforced so that he has a chance of preserving his soul. In Galatians 3:24, we read:

*"Therefore, the law was our tutor to bring us to Christ, that we might be justified by faith."*

So, the assumption that we can better help the criminal by loosening the grip of the law on him is an error in judgment. Criminality did not become a reality here on earth when Lucifer or Satan was cast down to earth. Man would have to buy in on the idea. Jesus said in Luke 10:18:

*"And He said to them, "I saw Satan fall like lightning from heaven."*

This happened in eternity past, even before the creation of man. After man was created, we do not have any time frame provided, regarding the period past before Satan approached man to turn him into a criminal. According to the biblical text, to tempt man to turn him into a sinner is the same as turning him into a criminal. There are two ways available to mankind. which can be used to rehabilitate sinners and criminals. One is for an individual to accept God's grace, as provided in the Lord Jesus Christ, who will change this person's heart from guilty under the law, into the righteousness of God, as Saint Paul states:

*"Therefore, if anyone is in Christ, he is a new creation; old things have passed away; behold, all things have become new."* And *"For He made Him who knew no sin to be sin for us, that we might become the righteousness of God in Him."* (II Corinthians 5:17, 21).

Or two, the criminal gets arrested by the police, and then is forced to make amends with society through man's legal justice system. That's it! The laws of human society, when understood from a spiritual perspective, are not for destruction, but are extremely beneficial. It can morally rehabilitate, which is the same as transforming a person's life. It can turn an individual's life around, bringing him back to the right path of morality, and he is then better positioned to receive the grace of God before it is too late. Obeying the law of the land does not save a person's soul, but places him in a correct position, facilitating the acceptance of salvation. That is what Saint Paul stated in his letter to the Galatians, saying:

*"Therefore the law was our tutor to bring us to Christ, that we might be justified by faith. But after faith has come, we are no longer under a tutor."*
(Galatians 3:24-25).

The officer of the law, even the arresting officer, when perceived correctly, becomes a helping angel himself. The same tasks performed by angels of God in the Old Testament can be performed by officers of the law in today's world. I will discuss that more specifically, further ahead. When the laws of man are applied toward an individual who has committed a crime, and if the individual will respond to it in compliance, it can help him to move toward God's saving grace. To neglect the application of the law is the same as letting the individual go completely toward perdition. Remember, the Code of Law is sacred, and most definitely serves a divine purpose. Obedience to the law of the land does not save a soul, but it helps to position the individual toward receiving the grace of God.

There is much to say about criminality, but the purpose of this work is to address this problem from the perspective of law enforcement personnel. I feel that the attacks on the police are unfair; it is not honest, and the fact that some people are using them for political gain is disgusting. It is not honest, because the laws they are enforcing are in the books, and if a police officer acts unlawfully, deal with him specifically, and in this way, we avoid attacking and demoralizing the entire police force. The intention to demoralize the police is an attack not only against law enforcement agencies, but it is also an attack against the Code of Law. To attack law enforcement and the Code of Law represents also an attack against the heart of the nation. If you defund the police, you remove your warriors, and without them, the Nation will be completely vulnerable to corruption.

Having a Code of Law which is compromised and with no serious intention to specifically deal with criminality, does provide criminality with the opportunity to sink its claws deeper into the American civilization, and it sets our society in the direction of doom. Yes, the Code of Law and its enforcement are that important.

One of the problems in our society comes from some of the district attorneys and even some of the judges that are taking a *laissez-faire* approach to criminality, and they are not prosecuting criminals to the full extent of the law. Police officers do their job, and make an arrest, but then the criminal is turned loose, many times to go back to the streets to commit other crimes.

Jesus, in Matthew 24:12, said:

*"And because lawlessness will abound, the love of many will grow cold."*

This statement, regarding lawlessness, was part of His prophetic sermon, and it provides insight into the emotional and psychological effects of criminality. It kills love, generates detachment between people, feeds on selfishness, and promotes hatred. Criminality carries the potential for aggression, violence, and murder. Jesus said that there would come a time upon the earth when it would increase, and such time may be here. And, if it is so, defunding the police will only promote more criminality, and therefore the defunding of the police would become a facilitator for the increase in crime. I will go to the point of saying that the movement to defund the police is in itself lawlessness. This social movement cannot be trusted, and certainly, those who are promoting it are not reliable people. This is a conspiracy against the safety of law-abiding people living in the community.

By defunding the police, you are taking my guardian angel away from me. Unless you are going to provide me with what I need to protect my own life, my property, my street, and my neighborhood. Any government agency that expects the people to provide for their own safety has lost common sense and is headed toward a state of total confusion.

## The Arrest of the Chief Criminal

When it comes to criminality, people have only one wish: crush it! If the criminal represents a threat to the safety of people, nothing is more desirable than to see such a criminal incarcerated. People lose sleep at night when their environment is not safe. People do not want to hear about being patient and tolerant toward those who are considered to be a menace to society. I have seen people, right here in America, acting hostile and aggressive during public manifestations, burning police cars, destroying private properties, ready to fight and be violent, and some of our leaders would not come out and condemn it. I am an immigrant, and I was appalled by the fact that our nation is losing touch with the true reality of what crime really is.

I am afraid America is under attack. A person might ask, under attack by whom or what? We are being attacked by the spirit of criminality, which is trying to destroy our values, trying to change our face from a law-abiding nation to a lawless one. We can pray to God, and we should, but He expects us to use the Code of Law and enforce it to curb the advancement of crime. God gave men authority, and if they won't use that authority lawfully, then why claim to have it? The Code of Law is a mechanism given to man so that when enforced, it becomes a means by which society can endure. This is the only way mankind has to stop the advancement of crime and immorality. God won't stop it, because he expects the proper authorities to deal with it, and to do so responsibly. Praying to God so He will put a stop to crime, won't work. He expects us to make use of both the authority He gave us as well as the Code of Law.

There is lawlessness, not just on earth, but in the entire universe. It has been dealt with in Heaven, and now it must be dealt with here on earth. The archetype of criminality, Lucifer, the fallen angel, is still on the loose here on earth. Choosing to ignore him or to talk as if there is no devil, won't change anything. This is a spiritual reality, and we just have to know how to deal with it. We can use the Bible to provide people with spiritual guidance, or we can use the Code of Law to provide them with moral guidance. Why is he still on earth? Man is to blame! When man allowed Lucifer to deceive him in the Garden of Eden, man gave Lucifer an extension of time in earth's environment.

Lucifer has been busy working in men and through men. That is how he got to share the dominion men were given on earth,

*"So, God created man in His own image; in the image of God He created him; male and female He created them. Then God blessed them, and God said to them, "Be fruitful and multiply; fill the earth and subdue it; have dominion over the fish of the sea, over the birds of the air, and over every living thing that moves on the earth."* (Genesis 1:27-28).

Mankind was given dominion, but then, through the temptation in the Garden of Eden, Lucifer got the stronghold that he needed to give him endurance. He is still illegal but remember that illegality is what he is all about. The fight against crime in Heaven is finished, and now, the fight against crime has to be fought here on earth! There is nowhere else! We need a Code of Law, and we need a law enforcement agency.

I believe that if mankind had denied him an entrance, he would have been finished. But now, we have to wait until God's time is completed, so Lucifer can be arrested and then locked up.

There is already a warrant for his arrest issued in the prophetic word, and that is what we have in the Book of Revelation 20:1-3,

*"Then I saw an angel coming down from heaven, having the key to the bottomless pit and a great chain in his hand. He laid hold of the dragon, that serpent of old, who is the Devil and Satan, and bound him for a thousand years; and he cast him into the bottomless pit, and shut him up, and set a seal on him, so that he should deceive the nations no more till the thousand years were finished. But after these things he must be released for a little while."*

Noticed the angel in John's vision who had the key to the bottomless pit, which is God's prison, and he also had a chain to bind Lucifer with, and then place him in the bottomless pit for a thousand years. With Lucifer in prison for a thousand years, if any human being commits a crime, it will be exclusively motivated by his human nature. The idea is that the place for all criminals is in county jails or prisons.

The angel that was sent to arrest Lucifer, served then as law enforcement personnel and can be referred to as a role model to the police officers we have today. Lucifer is a spiritual being, and only another spiritual being or angelic being could execute his arrest. We observe his actions on earth because some people have integrated and internalized his way of thinking. When people yield power to Lucifer, they become transgressors of 1) God's spiritual principles, and 2) they become transgressors of the laws of men. That is how this fallen angel can manifest himself on earth. This is a physical world, and spiritual beings can only manifest themselves in it through people. By dealing with the criminality of people, the Code of Law deals with the original crime of Lucifer, serving a divine purpose in that way.

There have been great efforts from men to disconnect earth from Heaven, and that is still going on even within the educational system. The struggle to determine how earth came about, if created by God, or if it was the result of a big bang or some other evolutionary process.

Mankind does not have the power to make such determinations. Remember, we are the creation, and we are the finite ones. We are allowed to daydream, but to isolate earth from its Creator? That is an impossible task, and the presence of criminality on the earth is in itself evidence of such a connection. After all, if a crime committed in Heaven sometime in eternity past, which was an act of rebellion toward God and his throne, is now being perpetrated on earth by rebellious people who continue to perpetuate that crime by thinking that they can take over the earth, and take over the affairs of humanity, and remove God from the scenes, that, to me, is a huge connection between Heaven and earth. We have that crime described in Isaiah 14:12-15 where we read,

*"How you are fallen from heaven, O Lucifer, son of the morning! How you are cut down to the ground, You who weakened the nations! For you have said in your heart: 'I will ascend into heaven, I will exalt my throne above the stars of God; I will also sit on the mount of the congregation On the farthest sides of the north; I will ascend above the heights of the clouds, I will be like the Most High.' Yet you shall be brought down to Sheol, to the lowest depths of the Pit."*

A segment of the human population is now trying to explain God away. And they don't see the presence of the archetype of criminality in what they are doing. I believe that Lucifer has been delusional since he decided to topple God, and now men are delusional by thinking that they can defeat God and move Him out of the way. God cannot be canceled! God will not allow Himself to be canceled!

There are three places in the universe where we have the presence of human activities: in Heaven, here on earth, and under the earth. The place under the earth is the place of the dead because they are separated from God, but they are not extinct. See the story of the rich man and Lazarus in Luke 16:22-26, where we read,

*"So it was that the beggar died, and was carried by the angels to Abraham's bosom. The rich man also died and was buried. And being in torment in Hades, he lifted up his eyes and saw Abraham afar off, and Lazarus in his bosom. "Then he cried and said, 'Father Abraham, have mercy on me, and send Lazarus that he may dip the tip of his finger in water and cool my tongue; for I am tormented in this flame.' But Abraham said, 'Son, remember that in your lifetime you received your good things, and likewise Lazarus evil things; but now he is comforted and you are tormented. And besides all this, between us and you there is a great gulf fixed, so that those who want to pass from here to you cannot, nor can those from there pass to us."*

The rich man was in hell, or the place of the dead, yet he could communicate with Father Abraham, who was on the side where the people of faith in the Old Testament went when they died. So, the human soul does not die, because the death of the soul is actually a reference to being eternally separated from the presence of God. In the Book of Revelation 5:1-3, John had a vision of a scroll held in the hand of God, which was sealed with seven seals, and nobody had been found worthy to open the scroll, and John wrote,

*"And I saw in the right hand of Him who sat on the throne a scroll written inside and on the back, sealed with seven seals. Then I saw a strong angel proclaiming with a loud voice, "Who is worthy to open the scroll and to loose its seals?" And no one in heaven or on the earth or under the earth was able to open the scroll, or to look at it."*

Notice, no one in Heaven, or earth, or under the earth was able to open the scroll, but the Lamb of God, Jesus Christ. These three realms are mentioned also in Philippians 2:10 where Saint Paul says,

*"That at the name of Jesus every knee should bow, of those in Heaven, and of those on earth, and of those under the earth."*

So, Heaven, earth, and under the earth are all connected, and it is not finite humanity which is the element that will be able to disconnect them.

Under the earth, we have those who suffered the consequences for their criminality here on earth. In Heaven, we have those who responsibly dealt with their crime by being law-abiding citizens, and by accepting the gracious gift of God in the Lord Jesus Christ. Here on earth, the fight against criminality still goes on.

# PART THREE

## The Fall of Human Civilization

This is a consideration that will address the destruction of two biblical civilizations. We are referring to the pre-diluvian generation and the cities of Sodom and Gomorrah. But, before we discuss what led to the destruction of these two civilizations, I have to take the time to make sure that people know that God was not the author of it. I know that some people are thinking that I have lost my marbles, but no, I am perfectly sane. Most people, if not all people have believed that God, out of his own initiative destroyed these civilizations. Someone might say, how about God's judgment? I can say right now that God's judgment is legal, and it is fair, and just, and it is dispensed as a consequence to those who have absolutely refused His gift of love. After the act of disobedience committed in the Garden of Eden, impending judgment became the norm.

First, let's take a look at what Saint James says:

*"Every good gift and every perfect gift is from above, and comes down from the Father of lights, with*

*whom there is no variation or shadow of turning."* (James 1:17).

This is a fact. Therefore, to say that God determined and initiated the process by which those two civilizations were destroyed is not accurate. It is an error of judgment.

Let's take some time here to explain what or who really brought death and destruction to the universe. Lucifer did. We have already seen how Jesus Christ referred to him as a thief and a killer, and that he comes only to destroy, as stated by Jesus himself, saying,

*"The thief does not come except to steal, and to kill, and to destroy. I have come that they may have life, and that they may have it more abundantly."* (John 10:10).

Now, let's take a look at what the Prophet Isaiah said about Lucifer, and we read *"Those who see you will gaze at you, and consider you, saying: 'Is this the man who made the earth tremble, who shook kingdoms, who made the world as a wilderness and destroyed its cities, who did not open the house of his prisoners?' "All the kings of the nations, all of them, sleep in glory, everyone in his own house; But you are cast out of your grave like an abominable branch, like the garment of those who are slain thrust through with a sword, who go down to the stones of the pit, like a corpse trodden underfoot. You will not be joined with them in burial, because you have destroyed your land and slain your people. The brood of evildoers shall never be named. Prepare slaughter for his children because of the iniquity of their fathers, lest they rise up and possess the land, and fill the face of the world with cities." (Isaiah 14:16-21).* So, who destroyed the cities, and who would refuse to open the house of his prisoners? In verse 20, we are informed about who destroyed his land and slayed his people. Who keeps the children under bondage because of the iniquities of their fathers (verse 21), and keeps them from possessing the land and building big cities? No, it was not God, but Lucifer. In Ezekiel 28:16, we read:

*"By the multitude of your merchandise they have filled your midst with violence, and you have sinned;"*

Here, the question should be, who is filled with violence? And the answer is Lucifer. Violence originated from his iniquities or his lawlessness.

So, people should not blame God. The blaming of God comes out of spiritual ignorance. One of the problems is that we actually have no idea what could really have happened to the planet, when Adam and Eve listened to Lucifer, and we read in Genesis 3:1-13,

*"Now the serpent was more cunning than any beast of the field which the Lord God had made. And he said to the woman, "Has God indeed said, 'You shall not eat of every tree of the garden'? And the woman said to the serpent, "We may eat the fruit of the trees of the garden; but*

139

*of the fruit of the tree which is in the midst of the garden, God has said, 'You shall not eat it, nor shall you touch it, lest you die.'" Then the serpent said to the woman, "You will not surely die. For God knows that in the day you eat of it your eyes will be opened, and you will be like God, knowing good and evil." So when the woman saw that the tree was good for food, that it was pleasant to the eyes, and a tree desirable to make one wise, she took of its fruit and ate. She also gave to her husband with her, and he ate. Then the eyes of both of them were opened, and they knew that they were naked; and they sewed fig leaves together and made themselves coverings. And they heard the sound of the Lord God walking in the garden in the cool of the day, and Adam and his wife hid themselves from the presence of the Lord God among the trees of the garden. Then the Lord God called to Adam and said to him, "Where are you?" So he said, "I heard Your voice in the garden, and I was afraid because I was naked; and I hid myself." And He said, "Who told you that you were naked? Have you eaten from the tree of which I commanded you that you should not eat?" Then the man said, "The woman whom You gave to be with me, she gave me of the tree, and I ate." And the Lord God said to the woman, "What is this you have done?" The woman said, "The serpent deceived me, and I ate."*

Because God immediately intervened on behalf of mankind, His intervention kept Adam and Eve alive and kept the Garden intact. How do I know that? I just read the Prophet Isaiah's description of Lucifer and I know that if left alone with Lucifer, and if God would not restrain Lucifer from doing what he could do, he would have killed the first couple, and destroyed the Garden of Eden. Why? Because he hates God, he hates mankind, and he is a thief, a killer, and a destroyer by what he has become: a criminal.

So, Lucifer is the primary culprit, and Adam and Eve are the secondary ones. The law of God in the Garden was, if you eat that fruit, you will certainly die! They broke that law and should have been dead physically, mentally, and spiritually, but because God had given them free will, it would not be right for God to see them dead when He gave them the ability to choose. That was the same dilemma God faced when Lucifer broke the law in Heaven. Now, God would have to hold together the loose ends really tightly to make sure that the worst would not happen: the destruction of the planet. How do I know that? Because I know that Lucifer is a merciless destroyer, and without divine supervision, he would have done it. He has been trying for approximately six thousand years now.

What no man knows is what really could have happened without divine intervention, and the reason we don't know is that God did not allow it to happen. Our problem is that we only know the facts, after the facts, because we are not prophets. And, if a particular event has not occurred, then we think that not even its possibility existed. The only reality we know is that which is historic and that which is present. How about the future? It is good that we don't know the future because it would cause a great number of people to have a heart attack!

The whole planet earth is marked for destruction if left unredeemed. God will purify it through the fire. Saint Peter says,

*"But the day of the Lord will come as a thief in the night, in which the heavens will pass away with a great noise, and the elements will melt with fervent heat; both the earth and the works that are in it will be burned up."* (II Peter 3:10).

That is how God purifies the elements; He uses fire.

## God's Unwritten Laws

We know very little about the unwritten laws of the universe. God had placed a hedge of protection over and around everything, after the fall of man. This protection provided by God has kept the whole environment from total collapse. The earth and the environment around it are actually extremely dangerous and susceptible to all kinds of catastrophic events. We still have tornados, hurricanes, and earthquakes, but they happen with restraint. If the restraining power was to be removed, then these most horrifying manifestations of nature would be ongoing, and the end would be imminent. What or who has caused it? Not God! Actually, God has been holding it all together until His times are completed. Who ensures that these unwritten laws are not violated? The angels of God do! They are the police of the universe. These angels are God's enforcers of the unwritten laws. There are a lot of people concerned with global warming, but don't worry, it may get hot, but not as hot as you think, at least not yet! If the sun were to move one inch closer to our planet, chances are we would all burn, but the sun is governed by God's unwritten laws, and he has angels patrolling the universe making sure that Lucifer and his criminal angels do not precipitate events that would cause life on earth to be unbearable.

There are a lot of things that people do not know about, yet they think they do. And believe it or not, they should be thankful to God that they don't know it all! Not knowing it all saves people from unbearable stress. And God will not allow mankind to destroy the planet either. Mankind is actually helpless. We are either under the mercy of God, or we are under the gun of Lucifer. We ought to be turning to God, and because we refuse to turn to God, the earth has become Lucifer's playground.

The water we drink is H2O, meaning that each of its molecules contains one part oxygen and two parts hydrogen atoms. You have heard of the split of hydrogen and oxygen atoms to create a nuclear bomb. These bombs could cause a great deal of destruction, but God will not allow it to happen. Lucifer certainly wants it to! The air we breathe is 2 parts nitrogen and 2 parts oxygen, and if that formula were to be altered, chances are that the whole environment, including the earth, would explode. Who makes sure that this formula is not disturbed? God does! So, the bottom line is, we live in a universe that is a billion times more dangerous than a powder keg. But the angels of God police the universe, keeping an eye on the criminal angels to make sure that Lucifer's destructive plans are kept restrained. If God were to remove his hedge of protection away from the earth, and mankind, there is a great possibility that we would be immediately annihilated. God does not kill people, He does not destroy things; much to the contrary, He has always been focused on preserving everything.

Man's journey in this universe is like taking a walk through the woods which have thousands of poisonous snakes around, but because these snakes are unseen, it causes man to feel overly confident and in control. In chapter 6 of the Book of Revelation, we have the opening of the seals and all other events that come after it. Let me present that chapter in the following way:

verse 2, "And I looked, and behold a white horse. He who sat on it had a bow; and a crown was given to him, and he went out to conquer." This is Jesus who now shows up authorized by the courts in Heaven to enforce the law on earth. Daniel saw when Jesus, the Son of Man, appeared before God the Father in Heaven, and Daniel testifies:

*"I was watching in the night visions, and behold, one like the Son of Man, coming with the clouds of heaven! He came to the Ancient of Days, and they brought Him near before Him. Then to Him was given dominion and glory and a kingdom, that all peoples, nations, and languages should serve Him. His dominion is an everlasting dominion, which shall not pass away, and His kingdom the one which shall not be destroyed."* (Daniel 7:13-14).

Jesus is legal, he is the redeemer, he is the Lord of all Lords, but he is also God's highest lawman. In I John 3:8 we read,

*"He who sins is of the devil, for the devil has sinned from the beginning. For this purpose, the Son of God*

*was manifested, that He might destroy the works of the devil."*

Here, in this text, we see Jesus coming to destroy the works of the devil. What is his work? Criminality! He is the most skilled criminal in the entire universe. In the vision of Daniel, Jesus, as the Son of Man, appears before the Father to receive the authority to come into this world, and defeat Lucifer, the archetype of criminality. The criminal has been under restraint because if let loose on his own, he would have destroyed humanity by now.

What we have in Revelation 6, is the beginning of the unleashing of all that darkness has, to attack God and life on the earth, and it will, at that time, come without restraint. If it were not for the restraining power of God, all the plagues and pestilences of Revelation would have happened six thousand years ago. Lucifer knows God has established His plan for humanity within the frame of time, and if Lucifer could interfere with God's plan, to not allow God to hold the elements together until the completion of the times, then God would have been defeated. Mankind knows about wars, and many people have seen the horrors of wars, but they know nothing about spiritual warfare. Spiritual warfare happens 24/7, with the angels of God policing the atmosphere, watching the principalities and powers in dark places, making sure their destructive power is kept under control, as explained in Ephesians 6:12 saying:

*"For we do not wrestle against flesh and blood, but against principalities, against powers, against the rulers of the darkness of this age, against spiritual hosts of wickedness in the heavenly places."*

Now, in Revelation 6:2, Jesus starts the process by which the criminality of devils and men will be annihilated. So, the first seal brings in the Lord Jesus Christ, setting into motion the beginning of the process by which God will purge the earth, and get rid of the lawless one.

The other 6 seals are:

Seal #2, The Fiery Red Horse. Verse 3-4, *"When He opened the second seal, I heard the second living creature saying, "Come and see." Another horse, fiery red, went out. And it was granted to the one who sat on it to take peace from the earth, and that people should kill one another; and there was given to him a great sword."* This is going to be a horrible time on the earth, with people profoundly disturbed, upset, frustrated, and angry to the point in which there will be a wave of homicides. People will kill people over nothing, and that is what the principalities and powers and the rulers of the darkness (see Ephesians 6:12), have always wanted to accomplish on earth, but could not, due to the restraining power of God. The rider of this horse is a demon. He is ready to make use of the sword given to him and will start this horrible wave of homicide between human beings.

Seal #3, The Black Horse. Verses 5-6, *"When He opened the third seal, I heard the third living creature say, 'Come and see. 'So I looked, and behold, a black horse, and he who sat on it had a pair of scales in his hand. And I heard a voice in the midst of the four living creatures saying, 'a quart of wheat for a denarius, and three quarts of barley for a denarius, and do not harm the oil and the wine."* This black horse, with another demon on it, received permission to establish a shortage of grains on the earth. This elevation of the price of barley and wheat indicates a time on earth when there will be little food available, thus the high prices mentioned here. This demon is a demon that enjoys seeing people die of starvation. He has been active on earth, but so far with great limitation, and with the opening of this third seal, he will have his way.

Seal #4, Widespread Death on Earth. Verses 7-8, *"When He opened the fourth seal, I heard the voice of the fourth living creature saying, "Come and see. "So I looked, and behold, a pale horse. And the name of him who sat on it was Death, and Hades followed with him. And power was given to them over a fourth of the earth, to kill with sword, with hunger, with death, and by the beasts of the earth."* Here, all hell breaks loose! This horse carries a demon so powerful that his name is Death, and another demon called Hades is his follower. This is going to be a time of great darkness on earth, with these two demons receiving power over a fourth of the earth to kill people with swords, hunger, and wild animals.

Seal #5, The Cry of the Martyrs. Verses 9-11, *"When He opened the fifth seal, I saw under the altar the souls of those who had been slain for the word of God and for the testimony which they held. And they cried with a loud voice, saying, "How long, O Lord, holy and true, until You judge and avenge our blood on those who dwell on the earth?" Then a white robe was given to each of them; and it was said to them that they should rest a little while longer, until both the number of their fellow servants and their brethren, who would be killed as they were, was completed."*

This seal changes the flow of things a bit. It takes us as far back as two thousand years ago, when it started, and takes us to the end of this present dispensation, taking into consideration all the followers of Christ that died because of their faith in Him. Their deaths were the result of individuals in positions of authority, either political authority or religious authority, but that were influenced by the principalities and powers of darkness. And now they are crying out to God and seeking the punishment of Lucifer and his followers. They want justice. There are demons right now, which are kept in darkness and under restraint, but if they had their way, every follower of Christ would die the most horrible death possible.

The Author of Hebrews presents us with an excellent background regarding these horrific attacks on the people of faith. In Hebrews 11:32-38 we read, "*And what more shall I say? For the time would fail me to tell of Gideon and Barak and Samson and Jephthah, also of David and Samuel and the prophets: who through faith subdued kingdoms, worked righteousness, obtained promises, stopped the mouths of lions, quenched the violence of fire, escaped the edge of the sword, out of weakness were made strong, became valiant in battle, turned to flight the armies of the aliens. Women received their dead raised to life again. Others were tortured, not accepting deliverance, that they might obtain a better resurrection. Still others had trial of mockings and scourgings, yes, and of chains and imprisonment. They were stoned, they were sawn in two, were tempted, were slain with the sword. They wandered about in sheepskins and goatskins, being destitute, afflicted, tormented— of whom the world was not worthy. They wandered in deserts and mountains, in dens and caves of the earth.*"

Seal #6, Cosmic Disturbances. Verses 12-17, "*I looked when He opened the sixth seal, and behold, there was a great earthquake; and the sun became black as sackcloth of hair, and the moon became like blood. And the stars of heaven fell to the earth, as a fig tree drops its late figs when it is shaken by a mighty wind. Then the sky receded as a scroll when it is rolled up, and every mountain and island was moved out of its place. And the kings of the earth, the great men, the rich men, the commanders, the mighty men, every slave and every free man, hid themselves in the caves and in the rocks of the mountains, and said to the mountains and rocks, "Fall on us and hide us from the face of Him who sits on the throne and from the wrath of the Lamb! For the great day of His wrath has come, and who is able to stand?"*

The opening of this seal will bring a time on earth, that will cause the best of mankind to feel so horrified, that even death will feel like a relief. Stars will fall toward the earth, and it is probably a reference to the earth being hit multiple times by meteorites. I submit that there are demons, like now, that if they would be allowed, would guide meteors toward the earth to destroy it. These demons are powerful beings, and I continue to propose to you that, if it were not for the protection of God, and His restraining power, planet earth would have been completely devastated a long time ago.

Seal #7, The Seven Trumpets. Revelation 8:1-2, *"When He opened the seventh seal, there was silence in heaven for about half an hour. And I saw the seven angels who stand before God, and to them were given seven trumpets."*

The opening of these seals indicates the removal of the restraining power of God, keeping the door open for demons to come out of darkness, and onto the earth to create conflict and take peace away. Without the restraining power of God, these demons would have been released a long time ago, and the purpose of Lucifer and his demons is to create conditions in which life on earth can no longer be sustained, therefore causing God to have failed to maintain His own creation.

God has used His power to keep these destructive forces from prevailing, but the sinfulness of men has also become unbearable to God. So now, it is God's turn to call His angels and put them in standby mode, and so the criminals of this universe, Lucifer and his fallen angels can bring destruction to earth on a scale never previously seen by mankind. Revelation 16:8-9 says:

*"Then the fourth angel poured out his bowl on the sun, and power was given to him to scorch men with fire. And men were scorched with great heat, and they blasphemed the name of God who has power over these plagues; and they did not repent and give Him glory."*

The only reason for global warming, in this case, is the fact that mankind has not acknowledged God, and given Him glory. The sinfulness of men is the reason because they have chosen to neglect God, and to deny His Christ and His word. God has restrained Lucifer's destructive intentions, and He has preserved humanity for as long as He possibly could, but now, God is bringing the dispensation of the disobedience of men to a close, and He has removed some of His restraining power, although maintaining some control over these events, so Lucifer does not destroy every human life on earth.

The Book of Revelation, besides the Seven Seals, also has the Seven Trumpets (Revelation 8:6-10:11), and the Seven Plagues/Vials releasing the wrath of God on unrepentant mankind, (Revelation 15-16). And although these vials contain what is referred to as the "wrath of God," and they release on earth extremely destructive plagues, they represent God allowing those who rejected His salvation plan to reap the results of the choices they have made in this life. In other words, those who have chosen darkness will receive the consequences of their choice. They wanted darkness, now they can have plenty of it.

When we consider all the destructive powers unleashed by the opening of the Seven Seals, what happened on earth when the Seven Trumpets sounded, and then the Seven Plagues/Vials, we have to conclude that none of these elements originated in the Kingdom of

God. These plagues, sicknesses, and diseases originate in the realm of darkness where principalities and powers of darkness rule, (Ephesians 6:12). Also, James 1:17 states:

*"Every good gift and every perfect gift is from above, and comes down from the Father of lights, with whom is no variableness, neither shadow of turning."*

We maintain the notion that God does no evil or harm to the earth or man, and He has restricted that which the kingdom of darkness can do. All the evil unleashed on earth, as we have depicted in the Book of Revelation, was first conceived in the mind and heart of the archetype of criminality, Lucifer.

God is not the author of these destructive elements, and He could not have kept the earth from these catastrophic events because mankind had betrayed God and shared with Lucifer the dominion which God had given to men on earth, thus forming a partnership with the master criminal. God limited them as much as He could, but He could not keep these judgments completely from happening.

We must not forget about who the criminal is, and that,

*"The thief does not come except to kill, to steal, and to destroy."* (John 10:10).

In the Book of Isaiah, we have a description of his destructive influence, as unleashed on the earth, and we read:

*"Those who see you stare at you, they*
*ponder your fate:*
*"Is this the man who shook the earth and*
*made kingdoms tremble,*
*the man who made the world a wilderness,*
*who overthrew its cities*
*and would not let his captives go home?"*
(Isaiah 14:16-17).

The declaration "he made the world a wilderness," and "overthrew its cities," is a strong indication of who the destroyer is. There are two main culprits on earth, Lucifer and man. Lucifer, because he committed the first crime in the universe and man because he allowed this criminal to separate him from God, the Creator. In Revelations, we have the process of judgment by which God brings to an end the disobedience of mankind and Lucifer's life of crime in the entire universe.

All the plagues, the sickness and diseases, and all catastrophic events such as earthquakes, tornados, hurricanes, etc., are all manifestations of his criminality. He is the lawbreaker. It is in his nature to break the laws of God, the laws of nature, and he is the principal influence in men transgressing against the laws of society.

# Crime and Death

*"···but of the tree of the knowledge of good and evil you shall not eat, for in the day that you eat of it you shall surely die."* (Genesis 2:17).

What does this statement represent? It represents law and order. There cannot be any place in this entire universe in which law and order must not prevail. It must be the standard even in Paradise, or in God's Garden. Law and order are the only means by which human civilization can endure. Because criminality has totally permeated the environment is the reason that law and order have become so essential.

Lucifer is prowling around the Garden, and he brings criminality with him, and God knows man is a target. There is the reality of light and darkness, with both realms existing around man, and God must give man a law that will serve as a guiding light. Man will have to make a decision, not because God would force him to do so, but because the dangers of his environment, even in Paradise, would bring man to a place in which he would have to decide if he follows God, or Lucifer, the criminal.

All man had to do was say no to Lucifer. Do not follow the words of a criminal, because there is no credibility in them. And anyone following the words of a criminal will also become a criminal.

Crime, after it was committed in Heaven, led to the advent of darkness, and darkness means spiritual death. This was not just an appearance of a shadow or a dark spot somewhere in the universe, this was far more than that. This became a new realm, a place where the opposite of God and everything contrary to God, would exist there. This would be a place where there is no law and order and is, therefore, home to chaos. Man, who had been connected to the light of God, would now become connected to this world of darkness, and his state of being and environment was about to change dramatically.

No, man had no idea how much criminality would affect him and his world, and there is a great segment of society, even today, who continues to demonstrate that same ignorance. America is changing, and the number one problem in America is not financial. No, financial problems are not what will bring America to the ground, because Americans are too sharp in the matter of money, and they know how to manage their finances, but when the Code of Law is tampered with, then the darkness is about to get more intense. When law enforcement personnel are depicted as being the bad element, then that is already an indication that darkness is prevailing. Now, America, the paradise of the modern world, is losing its guiding light, which is the Code of Law.

If Adam and Eve wanted to keep the Garden of Eden as their home and keep the earth a place of blessings, they would have obeyed the law. All they had to do was to keep the law of the land, and they would have been fine. The same principle applies to life in America: keep the law of the land as it is written, and everything will be fine. But when the law and those who are sworn in to uphold the law are treated with contempt, that is an indication to us that one more nation of men is headed toward destruction.

What happened in the Garden? Death came in, affecting the reality of mankind, in a very profound manner. Everything would now be going through the process of deterioration, and man would become severely limited in that which he could accomplish. The ground, which up to this point only produced what was good, now would also start producing brier and other weeds, not just useless for consumption, but which also, if without control, would choke good plants. Death and dying came in many different forms. Anything left uncared for eventually will die, and that is the norm in nature, with the exception of those plants considered to be plagues. These can grow anywhere, and they can survive on their own unless aggressively combated.

When a plant is planted in the ground, it must be cared for or it will die, and even a human life that is brought into this world, if left without the proper care, death will be the result. To live requires work, dedication, nurturing, and diligence. To die takes doing nothing about it, and just letting it be.

Criminality is darkness, and death is also darkness. This is spiritual darkness, and most of humanity fails to understand that darkness is all around us and that God has been busy keeping it under restraint. This is what Saint John said,

*"In Him life, and the life was the light of men. And the light shines in the darkness, and the darkness did not comprehend not."* (John 1:4-5).

This spiritual darkness is a reality way beyond the comprehension of those people who lack spiritual insight. The commission of a crime in Heaven, and then men acting on the suggestions of Lucifer, opened the door for this darkness to penetrate the reality of mankind. Who is the culprit? Both Lucifer and man, not God!

In the Gospel of Matthew, we have the incident in which Jesus cursed the fig tree, causing it to die. At least, that is the way it reads, but Jesus did not curse the fig tree out of His own volition, thus killing it. What happened, then? You see, the planet is already cursed because of the sin of humanity, and therefore, the life present on the entire planet is already at risk, and if God were to remove the protection He has placed around it, life, just as the example of the fig tree, would come under the curse, and die. God told Adam and Eve, the day they ate of it, they would die, and everything else would die with them. Adam and Eve ignored God's words and became attentive to the archetype of criminality. The law of God to man, as given in the Garden of Eden, was very specific, and required no special interpretation, just obedience. However, if any particular aspect of the law of God needs clarification, Lucifer is not the one people want to rely on for such clarification.

When they acknowledged what Lucifer had to say, they also allowed him to influence them, but the worst outcome from this interaction between man and Lucifer is that Lucifer succeeded in gaining a place in the affairs of men. The truth is that if we can visualize this entire universe having a door giving entrance to it, and immediately outside that door is death, ready to enter, but with God keeping it outside. In the case of the fig tree, all that Jesus did was speak words that caused the hedge of protection around the tree to be removed, and automatically death took over.

Job is a great example we have when it comes to the protection that God has provided. While we are looking at God and blaming Him for death and dying, Lucifer keeps continuity to that which he does best, killing, stealing, and destroying. It was Lucifer who told God about Job,

*"So Satan answered the Lord and said, "Does Job fear God for nothing? Have You not made a hedge around him, around his household, and around all that he has on every side? You have blessed the work of his hands, and his possessions have increased in the land. But now, stretch out Your hand and touch all that he has, and he will surely curse You to Your face!"* (Job 1:9-11). Lucifer knew that all God had to do was to remove the layer of protection around Job and his family, and hell would break loose. So, God did partially remove the hedge of protection, but kept the layer of protection around Job's person, as we read in Job 1:12,

*"And the Lord said to Satan, "Behold, all that he has is in your power; only do not lay a hand on his person."*

Job's reality is the reality of us all. The idea that God is judgmental and destructive is the greatest misconception, in the entire universe. This misconception is the result of a lack of knowledge about God, and who He is. Lucifer is a master deceiver, and he has convinced a great segment of humanity that God is the problem. Saint Paul said:

*"And no wonder! For Satan himself transforms himself into an angel of light."* (II Corinthians 11:14).

God's Judgment. In Romans 1:26-32 we read,

*"For this reason, God gave them up to vile passions. For even their women exchanged the natural use for what is against nature. Likewise, also the men, leaving the natural use of the woman, burned in their lust for one another, men with men committing what is shameful, and receiving in themselves the penalty of their error which was due. And even as they did not like to retain God in their knowledge, God gave them over to a debased mind, to do those things which are not fitting; being filled with all unrighteousness, sexual immorality, wickedness, covetousness, maliciousness; full of envy, murder, strife, deceit, evil-mindedness; they are whisperers, backbiters, haters of God, violent, proud, boasters, inventors of evil things, disobedient to parents, undiscerning, untrustworthy, unloving, unforgiving, unmerciful; who, knowing the righteous judgment of God, that those who practice such things are deserving of death, not only do the same but also approve of those who practice them."*

God never extends His hand toward people to harm them, and in this particular text, all that God did was leave people alone. In other words, if this is the way people want to live their lives, then so be it! The deterioration of life and the emotional and psychological consequences follow automatically. It is as if God were saying "You don't want me around, so I am leaving you to yourselves." Their demise is the result of the choices they made.

This text also shows us that without God's restraining power, the morality of men will only suffer further deterioration. Here, the text in verse 27 tells us that they received "*in themselves the penalty for their error.*" Their condition as human beings arrived at a state of misery never experienced before. In other words, all hell broke loose within them. God did not hurt them, all He did was to leave them alone, exactly as they wanted Him to. A great segment of the human population is ignorant about the extent of their need for God. They have no idea, and so many of these people just refuse to acknowledge how much they need Him, and they continue to exist due to His mercy, as we read in Lamentations 3:22-23, saying,

"*Through the Lord's mercies we are not consumed, because His compassions fail not. They are new every morning; Great is Your faithfulness.*"

David, in Psalms 41:1-5, said,

"*Blessed is he who considers the poor; the Lord will deliver him in time of trouble. The Lord will preserve him and keep him alive, and he will be blessed on the earth; you will not deliver him to the will of his enemies. The Lord will strengthen him on his bed of illness; You will sustain him on his sickbed.*"

Notice that the Lord preserves, and in doing so, he holds the person under his protection, not allowing his enemies, which is Lucifer and his demons, to accomplish their will in this person's life. In verse 3, we see that one way for destruction to come to a human being is through the plagues of sickness and diseases. People do get sick, but they don't get as sick as they could get if the Lord were to remove His protection away from them. Sure, the presence of sicknesses and diseases plaguing the human person is bad enough, but it is not nearly as bad as it could get. The potential for people to get sick and diseased is far greater than they can imagine. If people were to use their intelligence for something really profitable, they would be smart and seek shelter in God. Intelligently, they would include God in their lives, instead of excluding Him.

David, the psalmist, is one of the best examples we have, even when he wrote Psalm 91. In this Psalm 91, verses 1 and 2, David describes the intelligent human being as follows:

*"He who dwells in the secret place of the Most-High shall abide under the shadow of the Almighty. I will say of the Lord, "He is my refuge and my fortress; My God, in Him I will trust."*

Here David also tells us that God is our protection against pestilences, plagues, dangers by night, and dangers by day, and He also protects us from the attacks of Lucifer and his demons. But this psalm also shows us all the threats that are concealed within the realm of spiritual darkness. Lucifer rules in that realm and considering that he is a killer and enjoys destroying life, the angels of God have to constantly police him, and restrain him from what he can do in the realm of the physical.

Again, people do not know, and actually have no way of knowing it, besides believing the word of God and what it says about the full extent of divine protection, as dispensed on behalf of mankind. David talks about *"You shall not be afraid of the terror by night, nor of the arrow that flies by day, nor of the pestilence that walks in darkness, nor of the destruction that lays waste at noonday."* (Psalm 91:5-6).

The perils of this life are constantly present, always ready to strike, if it were not for God's protection around us. And according to Psalm 91:10-11, our safety is assigned to guardian angels, and we read,

*"No evil shall befall you, nor shall any plague come near your dwelling; For He shall give His angels charge over you, to keep you in all your ways."*

I am convinced that we have absolutely no idea what it takes to keep us and our environment safe. And the only explanation for our safety is that angels police our universe in the same way, law enforcement police our streets and roads.

So, Lucifer is under restraint, or he would create great devastation all over the earth, including taking the lives of people. Have you ever wondered about the reason why there is no life on other planets? Only men are foolish enough to think that they can resolve that problem. Actually, men could resolve it if God were to help them. But it is not going to happen, because all the activities of this universe have been restricted to Heaven, earth, and under the earth. I am submitting to you that criminality in the universe led to the devastation of these other planets. I am not saying there were human beings on these other planets, but it is possible that there was life: water, air, and all kinds of plants. What I am saying is, humanity must be very careful with becoming arrogant, because we don't know it all, and we should be humble before God. Criminality has caused more damage to the entire universe than we can assess.

So, when talking about the fall of human civilization, even as it happened through the flood, or by a storm of brimstones, as it was in the case of Sodom and Gomorrah, we have to constantly remind people that destruction is always pending, especially for those who turn away from God. On earth, the transgressions of God's laws and men's laws will always work as a trigger for destruction, not because of any condition God has established, but because of Lucifer's rebellion in Heaven, and then Adam and Eve giving him a foothold here on earth. A great segment of humanity has been acting impulsively, by assuming that there are no consequences for their actions.

Let me repeat: God does not hurt people, people hurt themselves. Here we are, in the year of 2023, and people find themselves involved in their criminality. What criminality is that? The Luciferian one which is to organize an assault on God's throne, to take him down, and get Him out of our affairs. The same criminality was committed in Heaven, as described in Isaiah 14:12-15, stating:

*"How you are fallen from heaven, O Lucifer, son of the morning!*
*How you are cut down to the ground, You who weakened the nations!*
*For you have said in your heart: 'I will ascend into heaven, I will exalt my throne above the stars of God; I will also sit on the mount of the congregation*
*On the farthest sides of the north; I will ascend above the heights of the clouds, I will be like the Most High.' Yet you shall be brought down to Sheol, To the lowest depths of the Pit."*

Lucifer's influence upon mankind is becoming more accentuated, with people moving away from God by leaps and bounds.

This act of criminality by mankind is well delineated in Psalm 2:1-4, where we read:

*"Why do the nations rage, and the people plot a vain thing? The kings of the earth set themselves, and the rulers take counsel together, against the Lord and against His Anointed saying, let us break Their bonds in pieces and cast away their cords from us. He who sits in the heavens shall laugh; the Lord shall hold them in derision."*

This end-of-time rebellion against the Almighty God and His anointed, Jesus Christ, is already well advanced. Here in America, they have decided that God, the name of Jesus, and the Bible cannot be mentioned in public gatherings because it is offensive to some. So, America is moving from serving God to serving people. Political systems are more concerned with how some people feel than how God feels. I believe that everybody ought to have the freedom to talk about God, and/or their religious beliefs, anywhere, as long as they are not forcing that conversation on people who are not willing to have it. Many religious people need to become a little more sensitive to the fact that if someone does not want to hear about it, he/she should be left alone. I don't think God likes the idea of Him being forced on someone who does not want to hear about who He is. I understand that governing and ruling people are not easy tasks, but neither should it be that easy to rule against God.

A great segment of the population in the United States does not seem to know that their resistance to law enforcement is only an expression of their anti-Christ attitude. In that same way, those nations who would like to see the nation of Israel annihilated, are expressing their anti-Christ attitude. The more their anti-Christ disposition increases, the more anti-law they become. Why? Because they are also assimilating more of the Luciferian attitudes, and he is the real outlaw. Lucifer is using people, to maintain his rebellious movement against God. I am afraid that humanity is going head-on toward a crash into a concrete wall, and the concrete wall is God Himself. We cannot escape Him, and fighting Him is an impossibility, so, submit to Him!

## The Pre-Diluvian Civilization

It is always very dramatic and catastrophic when an entire civilization is wiped out. That civilization, the pre-diluvian one, underestimated all the dangers that resulted from the fall of humanity, as happened in the Garden of Eden, and as people are continuing to do. That civilization did not need to be extinct because they were given a chance to save themselves. They had enough warning, but they chose to ignore all the attempts on the part of God, to get them to acknowledge their transgressions. God used Noah and gave him a message that was exactly what that generation needed to hear. Again, most people that have read the biblical account of what happened, conclude that God, of His own volition, destroyed that civilization. Remember that the problem was criminality, and the problem with criminality affects humanity in two ways: morally and spiritually.

All human civilization can endure morality alone. I mean, that if people in certain civilizations choose to not acknowledge God, but they are law-abiding citizens, they can survive and do well, although they are still running a risk of losing the eternity of their souls. People don't go to Heaven because they are morally good, but because they have accepted the gift of God in the Lord Jesus Christ. But, by being lawful they can thrive and do very well. But, when people choose to do as they please, and have no regard for others, getting involved in a pattern of behavior that is marked by lewdness, then they are creating the conditions for destruction.

When decency no longer matters, and family life deteriorates due to the presence of violence, drug and alcohol abuse, and all types of sexual immorality, then the Code of

Law has had its arms shortened. Allowing people to do as they please and promoting the idea that "if it feels good, do it," is the same as pushing them further into moral decay. The Code of Law should never be perceived as too restrictive, because that would be the same as saying that fish spend too much time in the water. The legal code is supposed to be restrictive, and that is exactly why it exists.

Human beings, right now, are living as if they could endure forever with their own efforts. They do not think they need God or His word. People do not want to be inconvenienced by that which "the Bible says." So, we live carelessly, and we harden ourselves to the idea of a loving and saving God, and the less we hear about Him, the better we feel. That is exactly how the pre-diluvian civilization felt. Jesus Christ described it, saying:

*"But as the days of Noah were, so also will be the coming of the Son of Man be. For as in the days before the flood, they were eating and drinking, marrying and giving in marriage, until the day that Noah entered the ark. And did not know until the flood came and took them all away, so also will the coming of the Son of Man be."* (Matthew 24:37-39).

The pre-diluvian civilization did not know, but they followed the principles of Luciferian criminality, which is to forget God, ignore Him, remove Him from His throne, and be God yourself.

171

People are not going to listen, and they will grow worse to the point that when God removes his layer of protection from around them and their environment, they will hate God even more because their hearts will be so hardened. Let's take a look at that in the Book of Revelation, where we read:

*"But the rest of mankind, who were not killed by these plagues, did not repent of the works of their hands, that they should not worship demons, and idols of gold, silver, brass, stone, and wood, which can neither see nor hear nor walk. And they did not repent of their murders or their sorceries or their sexual immorality or their thefts."* (Revelation 9:20-21).

They will not be able to repent for all their transgressions. This is not just the description of people committing idolatry, but they are actually following demons, worshiping them, they are quick to murder other people, they are a generation of thieves, and criminality is their lifestyle. If there is not a Code of Law, and if there are no law enforcement agencies, it is exactly the way Lucifer likes it.

Now, let's ask the question about what really caused the flood. Saint Peter refers to Noah as a preacher of righteousness, saying,

*"And did not spare the ancient world, but saved Noah, one of eight people, a preacher of righteousness, bringing in the flood in the world of the ungodly."* (II Peter 2:5).

The word "ungodly," also means wicked, evil, and iniquity, which also means to live outside the law. That world was one completely controlled by crime, morally and spiritually. The family was greatly affected by that spirit of criminality and based on the words of Jesus in Matthew 24:37-39, they held weddings so they would have one more opportunity to eat, drink, and party. Marriage had no moral value, and it became a profane thing. By the way, that is what criminality does, it profanes the sacred and the holy.

In Genesis 6:5 it is stated:

*"And God saw that the wickedness of man was great in the earth, and that every imagination of the thoughts of his heart was only evil continually."*

The word "wickedness" is from the Hebrew word *Ra'* meaning, wicked, and evil in thoughts and actions; it means mischievous, malignant, noxious, injurious, hurtful, causing pain and unhappiness. It also means fierce and wild. So, we can see that in the definition of the word "wickedness," we have the description of what a criminal really is.

In Genesis Chapter 6:11-13 we read,

*"The earth also was corrupt before God; and the earth was filled with violence. And God said unto Noah, the end of all flesh is come before me; for the earth is filled with violence through them; and, behold, I will destroy them with the earth."*

The description of what had happened to that civilization continues in these two verses. Men had given in to a mentality of self-indulgence, immorality, and violence, which caused God to conclude that it could no longer go on. He would have to bring it to a complete halt. What the lord is having to deal with here is an indication to us of how important a Code of Law is, and also of its enforcement. If that civilization had had a sufficient Code of Law in place, and an efficient system of enforcing these laws, the severity of their moral decay could have been significantly minimized.

How can we characterize their criminality? Very simply, by completely ignoring God, so people don't have to be accountable to Him, and then, self-indulge by living only focused on the pleasures of the here and now. In this state of ungodliness and complete dedication to what is pleasing to oneself, we have two conditions that developed, and which added intensity to the deterioration of that society. The first one was the corruption of human conduct (immorality), and, secondly, the aggression and the violence that ensued: domestic violence, and violence out in the streets and other public places. When violence and aggression become prevalent, the strongest ones rule and bullies surface, intimidating everybody else inside the neighborhood. In this environment of lawlessness, sexual predators thrive, and individuals who are unable to protect themselves become the victims.

*"...the earth was filled with violence."*

This is the end of every society that dares to underestimate the Code of Law, which vilifies law enforcement agencies, or that allows these law enforcement agencies to become an instrument of political corruption. The pre-diluvian civilization did not have law enforcement agencies, and their laws, the little they had, were inadequate and mostly not written laws. In those days, man governed himself by his conscience, and conscience gets relatively easily corrupted, without specified and organized written laws. In the environment of lawlessness, Lucifer finds his playground, and immediately all sorts of criminal behaviors will surface. When Lucifer becomes the motivating element behind human behavior and considering he has no affection for any kind of life, he will lead people to their destruction. In the pre-diluvian civilization, there was no Code of Law, no law enforcement, and no 911 number available to be called.

In high crime areas, human nature expresses itself without any restraint, in which case there is always an increase in immorality and a concerning disregard for human life. The absence of law enforcement causes individuals to assume that they can violate the laws and get away with them. The absence of law enforcement or its restraining is the encouragement criminals are looking for. With the demoralization of law enforcement agencies, the conditions are right for individuals to feel they can do as they please, leading to a deterioration of societal life.

People who are law-abiding citizens are always the victims. They are usually victimized by unlawful and overpowering governments. When a system of government becomes corrupted, the people will suffer the consequences, but those who have a criminal mind will do what they do best: violate the rights of the law-abiding people, who end up being taken advantage of.

When a government system becomes overwhelmed by its need to control the masses, then they have assimilated Luciferian characteristics. This same government will make sure that they limit the recognition of God to a minimum, if not completely. Luciferian types of governments have no regard for human rights or human life. A Luciferian government always will find a way to "legally" favor the criminal. Or they keep their arms comfortably crossed while the criminals are in action. To become passive toward acts of criminality must be interpreted as a criminal act itself.

The flood is one piece of evidence that proves that life can't go on in such chaos. Therefore, the flood and the destruction of Sodom and Gomorrah are historical events to be noted and taken very seriously by all human beings. All human beings tend to try to get away from God. People, when unredeemed, are terrified even about the idea of God's proximity. They want to hide and fallen humanity is always living under the false impression that they can get by without God. Then, there is always that segment of the population that wants to get by without laws, only to find out that they are unable to maintain moral standards by conscience alone. Once they fail to acknowledge God, they go from bad to worse. Ignoring God, plus no established Code of Law, and with a segment of the population doing as they please, moral deterioration is inevitable.

Chaos is usually the result of the absence of the Code of Law, plus the absence of law enforcement agencies. Prior to the flood, there was neither. No human civilization can survive under these conditions. People are never safe outside of law and order because:

a) Individuals become extremely selfish

b) There is a major breakdown of the family system

c) Corruption occurs in the behavior of the general public, and that of the established authorities, leading to generalized abuses of power.

# Sodom and Gomorrah: What Caused it?

There are many critical areas attached to the problem of criminality, that many people are not willing to look at. One of those areas pertains to the spiritual aspect of criminality, and this is a crucial issue because spirituality is at the very core of life in the universe. Spirituality is the one topic that scares people the most. Most people, when considering the realm of spirituality, come face to face with the unknown. To them, it is an unknown, but spirituality is not out of their reach if they were only willing to directly deal with it. The spiritual realm can be divided into two different regions: light and darkness.

The region of light is governed by the Almighty God, as it is explained to us in I John 1:5 saying,

*"This is the message which we have heard from Him and declare to you, that God is light and in Him is no darkness at all."*

In the Gospel of John 1:4-5, we read,

*"In Him was life, and the life was the light of men. And the light shines in the darkness, and the darkness did not comprehend it."*

The realm of darkness is ruled by the principality of darkness, as Saint Paul explains:

*"For we do not wrestle against flesh and blood, but against principalities, against powers, against the rulers*

*of the darkness of this age, against spiritual hosts of wickedness in the heavenly places. "* (Ephesians 6:12).

Human behavior is affected by one or the other, all depending on what kind of decisions the individual has made internally. Saint Paul, in Romans 6:16, wrote: *"Do you not know that to whom you present yourselves slaves to obey, you are that one's slaves whom you obey, whether of sin leading to death, or of obedience leading to righteousness? "*

So, having a mindset of sinfulness, or criminality, will lead to the individual becoming completely dependent on sinning, or another way of putting it would be that the person becomes a servant of criminality. This mentality, without adequate intervention, will lead to destructiveness, just as we have in the example of the pre-diluvian generation, and also in Sodom and Gomorrah.

The reality of darkness and the reality of light exists, and human beings can only accept their existence, and then choose which one of those realms they want to have affecting their lives.

There is a great segment of humanity today, that would rather ignore the reality of light and darkness as if by ignoring it, it would no longer be there, which is just another delusion in our world today. Criminality is sin, and sin is darkness, and if not properly dealt with, will again cause the destruction of human civilization. There is a great number of people in a position of authority who think that by being nice to criminals, they can better control the problem of criminality. They are following the direction of the scientists or the researchers that are proponents of the behavior modification model and believe that the most efficient way to modify behavior is not to punish bad behavior, but to find positive ways to reward individuals who are behaving badly. People say that they can catch more flies with honey than with vinegar, but I say that dealing with criminals is not the same as dealing with flies. People can use honey if they want to catch more flies, but with criminals, the police are still your best option.

Let's consider what happened in Sodom and Gomorrah! In the Book of Ecclesiastes 1:9, we read,

*"The thing that has been, it is that which shall be; and that which is done is that which shall be done: and there is no new thing under the earth."*

Again, we keep making use of biblical information because we feel we are addressing people who have made up their minds that the Bible is by far more a hindrance to humanity than it is of any help. However, I want to believe that the reason I am using biblical texts, is because I believe that it is, in fact, the best source of historical information we have available to us. Biblical history is very relevant, and it helps us to know what lies ahead of us. Is there anyone wanting to know what the future brings? Read your Bible! So, the story of what happened to Sodom and Gomorrah should not be interpreted as being one piece of evidence of how mean and harmful God is, but rather to be taken as an example for the rest of us. God is God, and being holy, He demands accountability from people. Saint Peter says: *"And turning the cities of Sodom and Gomorrah into ashes condemned them with an overthrow, making them as example unto those who should after live ungodly."* (II Peter 2:6).

But humanity appears to be working itself around, and back to it. Why? Because humanity continues to reject information provided by God. People continue to follow the wrong type of lead and continue to fall for the same old Luciferian lies. They are going in the wrong direction, yet think they are correctly navigating their life.

Lucifer has succeeded in convincing a great segment of humanity, that God is the culprit when in reality he is the real troublemaker. Lucifer, the archetype of criminality, continues to perpetrate his crime, inconspicuously, as always. He has turned God into the bad guy in the eyes of people and has made God out to be the liar, deceiver, and hateful one. However, only God knows the reality of every human being, and what it takes to help them to get out of their spiritual predicament. Lucifer is the liar, and God is the truthful one. Lucifer declares that people should be allowed to do as they please, and God declares that lifestyle to be too dangerous a way to live life. God is for the Code of Law, and Lucifer has deceived people by convincing them that the Code of Law is too discriminatory, restrictive, and judgmental. God is for law and order, and Lucifer wants chaos. God is in favor of authority and government, and Lucifer wants people to be able to live under their own rule. A great segment of humanity, right now, is paving its road back to Sodom and Gomorrah, but they don't seem to know it. To them, this opinion could only come from a fanatical individual, a "square," or an ignorant conservative. The truth? Only time will be able to determine which.

The Garden of the Lord. The entire earth can be compared to a paradise. The earth is mostly beautiful, even the desert areas have details that are simply awesome. The only ugly thing on the earth is that which some people display in the form of criminality. Lucifer caused havoc in Heaven, the Lord got rid of him, and now he is here on earth, influencing people in an attempt to defeat God.

The Jordan Valley, an area of about 20 miles wide, between the Moab Hills, and the Judean Hills, was also as beautiful as paradise. We have a description of it, in Genesis 13:10 saying,

*"And Lot lifted up his eyes, and beheld all the plain of Jordan, that it was well watered everywhere, before*

*the Lord destroyed Sodom and Gomorrah, even as the garden of the Lord...*"

Notice the description "*as the garden of the Lord.*" That was before the destruction of Sodom and Gomorrah because after the destruction, that entire area became sterile, and most of it is now covered by the dead sea, where no life thrives. Think now, that this was one of the most beautiful spots on that side of the world, probably covered with green vegetation, trees, and clear streams of water, and then criminality came in, with crimes being committed, varying from littering the streets to the raping of men and women, and to homicides.

There was, in Sodom and Gomorrah, a group of men who thought they could get away with anything, and there was no law enforcement to stop them. The Code of Law was very limited, and the few laws they had were not being enforced. So, there was no restraint to criminality. Three thousand years ago or today, when criminality goes unrestrained, it does eat away at the environment around it like cancer.

When there is an effort in society to restrain the work of the police and to be a little more tolerant toward criminals, I believe, that is the beginning of beautiful cities becoming deprecated, and our streets covered with litter. Paradise is about to be turned into a disaster area. When the vandalism and the looting, and the desecration are done, one would think of it as a war zone. When the police are ordered to stand down and not get involved, barbarism takes over, and suddenly the most beautiful world, even the world of the United States, can become defaced and ugly.

In Genesis 13:13, we read,

*"But the men of Sodom were wicked and sinners before the Lord exceedingly."*

The terms *"wicked and sinners"* mean that they were criminals both before the Lord, and of course, before men. Between law and order and criminality, law and order must always prevail. Criminals, if they don't like the way the law treats them, have the choice to not break the law, and that is the only choice they should be given, and I believe that to be a fair proposition.

In the same way, people's transgressions get the attention of the Lord, and so does the work of law enforcement, which always should be that of restraining criminality. The Lord understands that unless criminality is curtailed, the safety of people becomes compromised, and He expects people in authority to act responsibly, and to create a system of law enforcement that is nothing but efficient.

In Sodom and Gomorrah, people were not safe, and no one dared to leave their homes after dark. At night, a group of individuals who were sexual predators was running on the streets of Sodom and Gomorrah. At least, that is what is described in the Book of Genesis, but I am assuming that they also had gangs of thieves, looters, and vandals running loose so that no one felt safe.

In the Book of Genesis 19:1, we see two angels arriving in Sodom. To the citizens of that city, these two angels were strangers passing by, and a group of sodomizers noticed them, and immediately they were lusting after them, not knowing they were angelical beings sent in to escort Lot and his family out of the condemned area. Lot had invited these two angels to stay in his house as his guests.

In Genesis 19:4-5, it says,

*"... the men of Sodom surrounded the house, both old and young," asking Lot "bring the two men out so that we may know them."*

Lot offered them his own two virgin daughters, which they refused and threatened to do even worse to him because they felt that Lot was standing in their way. So, these self-willed and ungovernable individuals, making serious threats to harm Lot, tried to grab him, but the two angels from inside the house reached out and getting hold of Lot, pulled him inside of the house. The angels then struck these men with blindness and neutralized them in that way.

What these men attempted to do to Lot and his visitors, represents a picture of unrestrained crime. These criminals were bold and daring, being almost sure they could get away even with murder.

This situation happened in a place once called Paradise, or the Garden of the Lord. It shows us that without law and its enforcement, even Paradise becomes an ugly place, not fit to live in! In time, the Most-High God steps in and allows the destruction of the place. If Sodom and Gomorrah had had an adequate Code of Law and active law enforcement agencies, chances are that the entire civilization could have been preserved. So, that is our evidence that the Code of Law and its enforcement is a major part of the survival of human civilization.

But let's take into consideration another biblical text, for us to be better able to pinpoint exactly why the place was destroyed. In the letter of II Peter 2:7-8, we read,

*"And delivered righteous Lot, who was oppressed by the filthy conduct of the wicked. For that righteous man dwelling among them, tormented his righteous soul from day to day by seeing and hearing their lawless deeds."*

Notice the mention of "their lawless deeds."

So, what destroyed that civilization? Unrestrained lawlessness, so, people had better pay attention now, and be very conscious of the holiness of God.

Saint Peter also points out the other harmful aspect of criminality saying,

*"And especially those who walk according to the flesh in the lust of uncleanness and despise authority.*

*They are presumptuous, self-willed. They are not afraid to speak evil of dignitaries.*" (II Peter 2:10).

Here we see unrestrained human nature, which is the mechanism that Lucifer uses to promote disorder and chaos. Lucifer wants people to do what pleases them, and inside each human being, there is a seed of rebellion against authority. It is the responsibility of the Code of Law and its enforcement to keep that rebellious tendency of people within legal boundaries.

If the higher authorities in the days of Sodom and Gomorrah had acted responsibly and had taken legal action against all the acts of immorality being openly practiced in those cities, then, possibly, the lives of many people could have been preserved.

The fact is, that out of the flood, only eight people were preserved: Noah and his family. Out of Sodom and Gomorrah, three people were preserved. The same condition that preserved the lives of these eleven people, a righteous and law-abiding attitude, could have served also to preserve the lives of everybody else. Truth is, no one had to die. These cities are still under the Dead Sea, and even today, nothing grows there. The Garden of the Lord, a place where people once dwelt and made their home, became a place of the dead, all because of the lawlessness of men. Therefore, we must place much emphasis on the Code of Law and its enforcement.

Regarding what happened to Sodom and Gomorrah, we must also bring into perspective the following: in the text of II Peter 2, verse 6, we read,

*"And turning the cities of Sodom and Gomorrah into ashes, condemned them to destruction, making them an example to those who afterward would live ungodly."*

Sodom and Gomorrah must be taken as an example by all human civilizations.

# The Luciferian Crime

What is the Luciferian crime? So many people are confused about it, and to so many other people, there is no such thing as a Luciferian crime, or they just don't believe that angelic beings exist. To many, God is the criminal, cursing fig trees, sending plagues, killing people, and sending them to hell, and He is the one destroying entire nations. To these people, God is the hater, and He is the real troublemaker, not Lucifer. These people do not understand that death and destruction, and the deterioration of everything on the earth started with the disobedience of man in the Garden, where man accepted Lucifer's deal by rejecting God's.

How common it has become for parents to blame God for the death of a child, blame God for their sickness and diseases, or blame God when they lose their homes or their wealth. How common to blame God for tornadoes, hurricanes, and earthquakes. Lucifer has succeeded in deceitfully convincing people that God is the culprit, thus turning all attention away from himself, the real criminal.

There was no darkness in the universe until Lucifer committed his crime as we have described in Isaiah 14:12-15, where we read:

*"How you are fallen from heaven, O Lucifer, son of the morning! How you are cut down to the ground, you who weakened the nations! For you have said in your heart: 'I will ascend into heaven, I will exalt my throne above the stars of God; I will also sit on the mount of the congregation on the farthest sides of the north; I will ascend above the heights of the clouds, I will be like the Most High.' Yet you shall be brought down to Sheol, to the lowest depths of the Pit."*

The darkness I am talking about is not regarding an area of the universe, where there is no light from the sun, but rather I am referring to spiritual darkness. This is the domain of evil, and in that realm, we find the reality of all elements that can kill, steal and destroy. This is Lucifer's domain, and he rules it. Saint Paul was referring to this particular domain when he said,

*"For we do not wrestle against flesh and blood, but against principalities, against powers, against the rulers*

*of the darkness of this age, against spiritual hosts of wickedness in the heavenly places."* (Ephesians 6:12).

In this area of darkness, Lucifer is the principal authority, and all other demons are under his command. The world has not yet known the full extent of his destructive powers because God has kept him under restraint.

One way God uses to keep Lucifer and his demons under restraint is by policing the universe. The angels that are obedient to God, the paramilitary angels, and the military angels are all endued with the responsibility to keep the entire universe safe. Scientists, such as astronomers, have done great work in exploring the vastness of our universe; they have discovered stars and planets, and continue to pursue further knowledge of it. However, there is one thing about the universe that people are yet ignorant of, and that is the risks that it represents to life on earth. One of those dangers is flying meteors hitting the earth, or the sun moving closer to, or too far from it.

On earth, we are always dealing with floods, droughts, extreme cold, or extreme heat, but never everywhere at the same time. Nature has a way to recover from its setbacks, and life always goes on. There is a power that keeps conditions from getting out of hand, and life on the planet remains relatively stable. We have had plagues, pestilences, and diseases that always take the lives of people, but never reach a point from which there is no return.

People do have a false notion about the reality of the universe. The reality of night and day, or dark time and light time on earth, is also a true representation of the entire universe. In human experience, darkness and light co-exist. Within each individual, determinations are made that lead to which realm is now more active, and in control of that person's life. This explains how so many people can be under the noonday sun, and still be in darkness because their thoughts are darkened due to the presence of the influence of the archetype of criminality, Lucifer.

People live their lives completely involved in the reality of darkness and light, and yet, most people have not had enough interest in either light or darkness to find out about its spiritual implications. People have absolutely no idea about the reality of darkness and light as an influence on people's thought patterns. People feel more comfortable living life on a superficial level, and even though they have formulated ideas and concepts, they continue to be reluctant to add spirituality to their views. Most people rest on the fact that they are religious.

Saint Paul, in II Corinthians 10:5, addresses the nature of human thoughts by saying,

*"For the weapons of our warfare are not carnal but mighty in God for pulling down strongholds, casting down arguments and every high thing that exalts itself*

*against the knowledge of God, bringing every thought into captivity to the obedience of Christ,"*

In this text, we have intellectual strongholds and arguments, and by "high thing," the Apostle is referring to those who think they know more than God Himself. There are millions of people inside the Christian church that have adopted political ideologies without the proper insight into what they really represent. People tend to rely on what they hear, and most people do not look any further. Even inside the Christian church, people rest on what they hear from the pulpit, and most do not have the determination to look any further. So, their spirituality is based on hearsay. That was Job's problem, as is described in Job 42:5, saying,

*"I have heard of You by the hearing of the ear, but now my eye sees You."*

So, when it comes to the true reality of life, people tend to live by feelings and impressions rather than in-depth experiences. Lucifer likes that. He wants people not to be sure of anything because not being sure is to keep an open door for all sorts of doubts. He has been challenging what people know, or think they know, from the very beginning of the human race. Notice how that whole conversation with people went, as we read in Genesis 3:1-7,

*"Now the serpent was more cunning than any beast of the field which the Lord God had made. And he said*

*to the woman, has God indeed said, you shall not eat of every tree of the garden'? And the woman said to the serpent, we may eat the fruit of the trees of the garden; but of the fruit of the tree which is in the midst of the garden, God has said, you shall not eat it, nor shall you touch it, lest you die. Then the serpent said to the woman, you will not surely die. For God knows that in the day you eat of it your eyes will be opened, and you will be like God, knowing good and evil. So, when the woman saw that the tree was good for food, that it was pleasant to the eyes, and a tree desirable to make one wise, she took of its fruit and ate. She also gave to her husband with her, and he ate. Then the eyes of both of them were opened, and they knew that they were naked; and they sewed fig leaves together and made themselves coverings."*

She was not sure of what God had said, was she? Notice, she had no argument to counter Lucifer with, contrary to the temptation of Jesus, as we have described in Matthew 4:1-11, saying,

*"Then Jesus was led up by the Spirit into the wilderness to be tempted by the devil. And when He had fasted forty days and forty nights, afterward He was hungry. Now when the tempter came to Him, he said, "If You are the Son of God, command that these stones become bread."*

*But He answered and said, "It is written, 'Man shall not live by bread alone, but by every word that proceeds from the mouth of God.'*

*Then the devil took Him up into the holy city, set Him on the pinnacle of the temple, and said to Him, "If You are the Son of God, throw Yourself down. For it is written:*

*'He shall give His angels charge over you,' and, 'In their hands they shall bear you up, Lest you dash your foot against a stone.*

*Jesus said to him, "It is written again, 'You shall not tempt the Lord your God."*

*Again, the devil took Him up on an exceedingly high mountain, and showed Him all the kingdoms of the world and their glory. And he said to Him, "All these things I will give You if You will fall down and worship me." Then Jesus said to him, "Away with you, Satan! For it is written, You shall worship the Lord your God, and Him only you shall serve.*

*Then the devil left Him, and behold,* angels *came and ministered to Him."*

Notice that Jesus was very sure of what he knew, and was, therefore, able to neutralize Lucifer's arguments. If people are only 85 percent sure, Lucifer is still satisfied, because he has a total of 15 percent to work with. That is why Jesus said that the first and great commandment is:

*"But when the Pharisees heard that He had silenced the Sadducees, they gathered together. Then one of them, a lawyer, asked Him a question, testing Him, and saying, "Teacher, which is the great commandment in the law?"*

*Jesus said to him, "'You shall love the Lord your God with all your heart, with all your soul, and with all your mind.' This is the first and great commandment."* (Matthew 22:34-38).

Notice that he is specific about all your heart, all your soul, and all your mind. Lucifer wants people to love, know, trust, and relate to God, only in part. To be dedicated to God 85 percent is only to the satisfaction of Lucifer, but not God. This criminal is super-sharp, and he is extremely capable of capitalizing on the smallest degree of weakness.

Lucifer loves to influence the way people think, and that is how he provides them with guidance, and also that is how he establishes strongholds within people's minds. He cannot perpetrate a crime within and around people unless he can affect their thinking patterns. Many people know how to fight with fists, feet, knives, swords, and guns, but too many people do not know how to fight thoughts with thoughts. That is what Jesus did when

Lucifer was trying to get into His mind. With Jesus, he failed, but with Eve in the Garden of Eden, he succeeded. He had to get inside the realm of her thoughts before he could provide her with guidance on what he wanted her to do.

Lucifer is now unable to commit his crimes unless he captures the thoughts of people. He is unable to manifest himself on the face of the earth unless he does so through people. A human being living his life against the determinations of the Code of Law is reflecting the darkness of Lucifer within human society. This person is living against the norms of man and God. He is lawless, and lawlessness is what it is, whether it transgresses the spiritual laws of God or the moral codes of man. Lawlessness is one and the same, as we have explained in I John 3:4, saying,

*"Whoever commits sin also commits lawlessness, and sin is lawlessness."*

Lucifer is the author of it, but he is unable to implement his criminality unless he first catches their attention. Lucifer is unable to turn a human being into a criminal, without first establishing a mental influence within that person, and then directing their thoughts. He talks the individual into the commission of a crime, and yet, he does not appear before a judge in a court of law, but the individual who broke the law does, of course.

Someone may say that since Lucifer is the culprit, and the influence leading the individual to commit a crime, so why punish the individual? The answer is that Lucifer is a spiritual influence, and as mentioned previously, he represents darkness. God, the Father of the Lord Jesus Christ, represents light, and He also is dependent on human beings to manifest Himself on earth. Human beings are agents, or instruments that can be used by either of those spiritual powers. However, human beings are not neutralized elements, and they are not robots either. Human beings are empowered by their own volition, and ultimately, they act upon a decision made internally, and that determines the nature of their action, whether of darkness or light. That is the reason Saint Paul states:

"*So, then each of us shall give account of himself to God.*" (Romans 14:12). Saint James states in the following way:

"*But each one is tempted when he is drawn away by his own desires and enticed. Then, when desire has conceived, it gives birth to sin; and sin, when it is full-grown, brings forth death.*" (James 1:14-15).

In verse 15, the word *sin* can be replaced by the word *lawlessness* because, in the New Testament, they carry the same meaning. In verse 14, the word *desire* can be replaced by the word *motivation*. But both desire and motivation must be processed internally, and then a course of action is chosen. If the individual is tempted to commit murder or rob a bank, that means he is coming under the influence of darkness. If he is enticed, that means he has yielded his willpower to the power of darkness. No! He is not possessed by Lucifer, but he is now under his influence. If this individual commits a crime, he will have to give account according to the law because as a human being, he has transgressed the laws of society.

Lucifer is already condemned before a court in Heaven, and his arrest has been recorded within the prophetic word, even as stated in Revelation 20:1-3, saying,

*"Then I saw an angel coming down from heaven, having the key to the bottomless pit and a great chain in his hand. He laid hold of the dragon, that serpent of old, who is the Devil and Satan, and bound him for a thousand years; and he cast him into the bottomless pit, and shut him up, and set a seal on him, so that he should deceive the nations no more till the thousand years were finished. But after these things he must be released for a little while."*

The bottomless pit is the prison where God puts all the unrepentant and unredeemed criminals, whether they are people or angelical beings. This text of Revelation 20:1-3 is the prophetic warrant of arrest issued for Lucifer.

Lucifer conceived lawlessness in his own heart. In Ezekiel 28:15, we read:

*"You were perfect in your ways from the day you were created, Till iniquity was found in you."*

The word *iniquity* means "lawlessness." It was conceived first within Lucifer's heart and mind, and therefore the concept of criminality did not exist within the universe prior to his fall. There was no spiritual darkness in the universe before that. The heartbeat of his crime is represented by an attack against the throne of God and constituted an attack against law and order in Heaven also. Lucifer continues to think that if he can prove God wrong, in even one word He has spoken, then he has won the conflict that he started in eternity past and would then become the ruler of the universe. At least, that is how this whole situation would develop from the perspective of a delusional mind. God will never, ever be caught in any compromising situation. His word is true, and it shall remain so for all eternity, just as we read in Matthew 24:35, where we read:

*"Heaven and earth will pass away, but My words will by no means pass away."*

Lucifer has attacked the integrity of God and will continue to do so because, as a criminal, he can only continue to practice criminality. He can't help himself, and until he is caught and locked up, he will continue to undermine the relationship that God desires to establish with all humanity.

Lucifer can only win within the boundaries of each human being. He can deceive people, causing them to reject God's love, and causing them to distrust His word, and in doing so, he will lead multitudes in the direction of darkness, and away from the light.

A great number of the human population, once deceived by Lucifer, will transgress the laws of God, and a segment of that will transgress against the laws of God and man, and these are the ones that law enforcement personnel have to deal with.

Let's categorize some of the implications of this assault on God's integrity, and upon humanity, as follows:

- Underestimating God. This is the action of the profane, Ezekiel 28:18 "...*Therefore I cast you as a profane thing...*" The profane is the one who has no affinities, and no respect for that which is sacred and holy.

- Thinking he could be like God, Isaiah 14:14 "*I will ascend above the heights of the clouds, I will be like the Most High.*"

- Wanting to establish a throne in Heaven with the purpose, I believe, of removing God. He thought he could cancel God in Heaven and is now attempting to cancel God on earth.

- Not wanting people to consider the Bible.
- Not wanting people to pray in public places.
- Not wanting people talking about Jesus.
- Not wanting people to be told that Jesus is the only Savior.
- Not wanting people to believe in absolutes, such as truth, and love and he wants more than just male and female, preferring that people keep an open mind to a third gender, and so on. He does not want marriage just to be between a man and a woman, but that it rather be between any two people, and gender boundaries are not to be taken into consideration.
- Wanting all religions to be considered equally important, and to be received as an equally effective means of resolving people's spiritual problems.
- With the same mindset, wanting the Bible not to be considered the absolute truth about the spirituality of people, and not wanting the Code of Law to be the absolute truth about human morality.
- Trying to turn Jesus into the villain; we see that initiative well characterized in the Gospel of John, where we read: *"Pilate then went out to them and said, "What accusation do you bring against this Man?" They answered and said to*

*him, "If He were not an evildoer, we would not have delivered Him up to you."* (John 18:29-30). Also, in John 19:6-7, we read: *"Therefore, when the chief priests and officers saw Him, they cried out, saying, "Crucify Him, crucify Him!" Pilate said to them, "You take Him and crucify Him, for I find no fault in Him." The Jews answered him, "We have a law, and according to our law He ought to die, because He made Himself the Son of God."*

And, in John 19:12, we read: *"From then on Pilate sought to release Him, but the Jews cried out, saying, "If you let this Man go, you are not Caesar's friend. Whoever makes himself a king speaks against Caesar."* Through it all there was this ongoing effort to attach to Jesus the image of a criminal, and Lucifer was behind it, influencing the thoughts of people in his attempt to turn Jesus from a worthy Lamb to an unworthy one. Remember, he had to be perfect, and being labeled a criminal could change all that, or at least, that is what Lucifer wanted to see happening, and the greater the number of people believing that the better he liked it.

- Attempting to make the church of God the enemy from the very beginning. In the Book of

Acts 8:1-3, we read: *"At that time a great persecution arose against the church which was at
Jerusalem; and they were all scattered throughout the regions of Judea and Samaria, except the
apostles. And devout men carried Stephen to his
burial, and made great lamentation over him. As
for Saul, he made havoc of the church, entering
every house, and dragging off men and women,
committing them to prison."*

* Continuing to perpetrate his crime, as he attempts
to turn humanity against God, His Christ, and His
church until he finally brings into the scenes, the
greatest human criminal ever; the antichrist. In
II Thessalonians 2:9-10, we read: *"The coming
of the lawless one is according to the working of
Satan, with all power, signs, and lying wonders,
and with all unrighteous deception among those
who perish, because they did not receive the love
of the truth, that they might be saved."* The antichrist represents Lucifer's ultimate criminal. If
there is ever a complete description of all that
a criminal is about, the antichrist would be the
epitome of it. Lucifer is extremely deceitful, and
the antichrist will represent his desperate attempt
to bring utter chaos onto the earth. Lucifer's antichrist character is also referred to in the Book

of Revelation, as the beast. In Revelation 13:4-6, we read: *"So they worshiped the dragon who gave authority to the beast; and they worshiped the beast, saying, "Who is like the beast? Who is able to make war with him?" And he was given a mouth speaking great things and blasphemies, and he was given authority to continue for forty-two months. Then he opened his mouth in blasphemy against God, to blaspheme His name, His tabernacle, and those who dwell in heaven."* So, the beast is given authority or is given the power of government to rule over all the nations of the earth and to unleash an attack against God, His name, His people, and against those who dwell in heaven. However, there must be no other option given to any criminal but to be apprehended and incarcerated, and that is exactly what will happen to Lucifer and his cohorts.

## Law and Order

When discussing law and order, I believe we are discussing one of the most important of all conditions within human society. Without law and order, we have chaos, and in chaos, human society cannot thrive. Safety is a very important element so that human growth can take place, and when law and order are not adequate, the environment becomes disrupted and unstable, and it negatively affects the well-being of people.

Law and order are extremely important, even for people to be able to sleep at night. If the environment is not safe, people become restless and emotionally upset. I am trying to remind people that the presence of law enforcement on our roads and streets is a necessity. Too many people are taking it for granted. I would say it is a part of our basic needs.

Abraham Maslow in his description of the hierarchy of human needs, developed the concept of a pyramid with people's basic needs being at the very bottom, and immediately above it, placed people's needs for safety, and above that he had the need to become, then esteem needs, and on the very top he had self-actualization, for those people who succeeded in having all these needs met as they went along in life. Mr. Maslow's insightful description of human needs becomes completely neutralized in communities in which the crime rate is high.

When people live in high-crime areas, they are more likely to be plagued by fear, or they are constantly living in a state of anger because they do not approve of the crime around them and feel helpless. After all, they are unable to make changes themselves. After all, people are dependent upon lawmakers and are aware that they cannot take the law into their own hands.

So, people can have water, food, a roof over their heads, plenty of money, and might even have a loving family, but if they live in a community that is plagued by crime, they will become dysfunctional and even unhealthy physically and emotionally. Therefore, there is no way for anyone to overemphasize the importance of law and order in the community, and for anyone to assume that communities around the country can do better with a smaller police force present out in the streets, is simply astounding.

Here is how it goes, fewer policemen on the streets, equals a higher crime rate. There is no way for people to have rest and peace of mind, in a neighborhood where crime is out of control. And I ask the question again, how important is the police force?

I believe that we cannot afford to have socialist people, who hold the idea that the best way to deal with crime is to hug and throw kisses at criminal individuals. Go ahead and throw them kisses, and they will throw knives and bullets back at you! This social idea that we have to be inclusive, instead of being judgmental regarding any particular segment of society, will go to the point where we compromise the Code of Law, to facilitate the life of the criminal. This socialist idea, if prevalent, could represent the damnation of entire civilizations of people.

True law and order call for the apprehension of criminals. What is true law and order? This is the law and order which reflects the integrity of the Code of Law. This is the law and order which is implemented by a police force totally dedicated to the safety of the community. This police force makes use of all legal means to apprehend those who represent any degree of risk to members of the community. This police force patrols the streets, detects the element of criminality, and then proceeds to bring it under control. This police force does not allow the element of defiance and rebellion to stop them, and they bring criminals under control nice and easily, when they submit, or are taken down by force when they try to resist arrest. This police force is out in the streets to protect the good folk of the community, and I add, they are out there to subjugate the bad element whether it is white, black, red, or yellow. Law and order should not be at the cost of the blood of innocent people. If the criminals do not like the way they are treated by the police, they have the option to not commit the crime!

The Bible says a lot about law and order. God is dedicated to law and order and He, Himself, had to fight crime in Heaven. During several millennia, Lucifer had access to Heaven, even after he attempted to take over

God's Throne as recorded in Isaiah 14:12-15, where we read:

> *"How you are fallen from heaven, O Lucifer, son of the morning!*
> *How you are cut down to the ground, you who weakened the nations!*
> *For you have said in your heart: I will ascend into heaven, I will exalt my throne above the stars of God; I will also sit on the mount of the congregation On the farthest sides of the north; I will ascend above the heights of the clouds, I will be like the Most High.' Yet you shall be brought down to Sheol, to the lowest depths of the Pit."*

It took more than fighting crime to rid Heaven of his presence, in fact, it was necessary to wage a war to force him out of Heaven, even as we read in Revelation 12:7-8, where we read:

> *"And war broke out in heaven: Michael and his angels fought with the dragon; and the dragon and his angels fought, but they did not prevail, nor was a place found for them in heaven any longer."*

They say that crime does not pay. It is true, it does not pay in Heaven, and it must not pay on earth. Lucifer used to be able to go into Heaven and make accusations against people, one of which is the story of Job.

According to the Book of Job 1:6-7, Lucifer went into Heaven and made accusations against Job, as we read:

*"Now there was a day when the sons of God came to present themselves before the Lord, and Satan also came among them. And the Lord said to Satan, "From where do you come?" So Satan answered the Lord and said, "From going to and fro on the earth, and from walking back and forth on it."*

In chapter 2:1-2, where we read:

*"Again there was a day when the sons of God came to present themselves before the Lord, and Satan came also among them to present himself before the Lord. And the Lord said to Satan, "From where do you come?" Satan answered the Lord and said, "From going to and from on the earth, and from walking back and forth on it."*

In both texts, Lucifer referred to here as Satan, stated that he had been walking up and down the earth. Lucifer, for reasons of his own, would blend in with the angels of God, and go into Heaven to make accusations against people. Was he allowed in Heaven? I say no, he was not, but as the criminal that he is, he kept violating boundaries that he was not permitted to. Criminals are defiant and rebellious.

The only explanation for his appearances is that, when Lucifer violated law and order in Heaven, he created a vulnerability in the heavenly realm that, although not allowed in, he still could go in, if that makes any sense. Lucifer's act of rebellion brought in the reality of spiritual darkness in Heaven, and until that darkness in the Heavens would be dealt with, he would have access to it. I am trying to point out that crime is a very serious problem. There must be no acceptance of it, and criminals must be made aware that criminal types of behavior are absolutely unacceptable.

One question to be asked is, does Lucifer still have the opportunity to go into the presence of God and accuse believers? No, he is no longer allowed to do that because that freedom was taken away from him. In Revelation 12:10, we read:

*"...for the accuser of our brethren, who accused them before our God day and night, has been cast down."*

The accuser of the believers was cast down, and now he would be confined to action within earth's atmosphere, for this environment has not yet been fully redeemed.

When would this darkness within the universe be dealt with? On the cross, two thousand years ago. The death and resurrection of Jesus Christ would have to reach way beyond the earth and under the earth. The author of the Book of Hebrews tells us that the blood of

Jesus had to be sprinkled in the tabernacle in Heaven, as we read in Hebrews 9:11-15, saying:

*"But Christ came as High Priest of the good things to come, with the greater and more perfect tabernacle not made with hands, that is, not of this creation. Not with the blood of goats and calves, but with His own blood He entered the Most Holy Place once for all, having obtained eternal redemption. For if the blood of bulls and goats and the ashes of a heifer, sprinkling the unclean, sanctifies for the purifying of the flesh, how much more shall the blood of Christ, who through the eternal Spirit offered Himself without spot to God, cleanse your conscience from dead works to serve the living God? And for this reason, He is the Mediator of the new covenant, by means of death, for the redemption of the transgressions under the first covenant, that those who are called may receive the promise of the eternal inheritance."*

So, the tabernacle in which the blood of Jesus was taken to, was not the one made by human hands here on the earth, but the one in Heaven. The Tabernacle erected on the earth, according to instructions given to Moses, was never touched by the blood of Jesus because fundamentally the problem with sin and criminality in the universe had come into reality not here on earth, but in Heaven. Law and order had first been disrupted in

Heaven, and in Heaven, it would have to be first dealt with by the blood of the Lord Jesus Christ. Lucifer hates the cross of Christ, and Saint Paul makes a good description of what happened there on Calvary, saying:

*"… having wiped out the handwriting of requirements that was against us, which was contrary to us. And He has taken it out of the way, having nailed it to the cross. Having disarmed principalities and powers, He made a public spectacle of them, triumphing over them in it."* (Colossians 2:14-15).

Law and order were reestablished in Heaven by Lucifer being completely removed from it. In Revelation 12:9 we read:

*"So the great dragon was cast out, that serpent of old, called the Devil and Satan, who deceives the whole world; he was cast to the earth, and his angels were cast out with him."*

Lucifer was cast out of Heaven, and onto the earth. After that defeat imposed on Lucifer by God's law enforcement force, the angels, there was a loud and great proclamation that could be heard in all the vastness of this universe, saying:

*"Then I heard a loud voice saying in heaven, "Now salvation, and strength, and the kingdom of our God, and the power of His Christ have come, for the accuser of our brethren, who accused them before our God day*

*and night, has been cast down. And they overcame him by the blood of the Lamb and by the word of their testimony, and they did not love their lives to the death."* (Revelation 12:10-11).

This is a great statement: "Now salvation, and strength, and the kingdom of our God, and the power of His Christ have come." Lucifer could not fight and win over that. Now, any human being wanting to overcome Lucifer has to do it based on the shed blood of the Lamb. This is the fight against spiritual criminality that is still going on here on earth.

The fact is that not only the believers overcame Lucifer by the blood of the Lamb of God, but Heaven overcame him also by that same blood. Jesus, on the cross, obtained a formidable victory for both Heaven and earth and under the earth because the saints of old had been kept captive for four thousand years waiting for the gates of hell to be busted, so they could ascend directly into the presence of God, as we read in Ephesians 4:7-10, saying,

*"But to each one of us grace was given according to the measure of Christ's gift. Therefore, He says: "When He ascended on high, He led captivity captive, And gave gifts to men." (Now this, "He ascended"— what does it mean but that He also first descended into the lower parts of the earth? He who descended is also*

213

*the One who ascended far above all the heavens, that He might fill all things.)"*

That is how God established law and order by sending His principal lawman, Jesus Christ, to set things right. But do not forget that Lucifer has been cast down to the earth, and here is where the fight against criminality still goes on. It goes on, on two different fronts: by the proclamation and teaching of the word of God, and by law enforcement personnel implementing the Code of Law constantly.

Law and order must always prevail, and for that to take place, there is a rule which applies to all criminals: ultimately, they must be apprehended and incarcerated. In Revelation 19:20, we have the description of the beast and his false prophet being apprehended, as we read: *"Then the beast was captured, and with him the false prophet who worked signs in his presence, by which he deceived those who received the mark of the beast and those who worshiped his image. These two were cast alive into the lake of fire burning with brimstone."*

Lucifer's arrest and imprisonment are recorded in Revelation 20:1-3, where we read:

*"Then I saw an angel coming down from heaven, having the key to the bottomless pit and a great chain in his hand. He laid hold of the dragon, that serpent of old, who is the Devil and Satan, and bound him for a*

*thousand years; and he cast him into the bottomless pit, and shut him up, and set a seal on him, so that he should deceive the nations no more till the thousand years were finished. But after these things he must be released for a little while."*

## Beliefs, Values, Virtues, and Criminality

Criminality is the one problem that is shared by all societies in the world. Crime exists wherever people can be found, and at this point in time, crime is proving to be a persistent, and out-of-control problem everywhere. Criminality is the single culprit in streets being unsafe; it is a fear-inducing element; it is an element of oppression, and it is the one evil that men do. Entire societies suffer from criminality because it victimizes people and also due to the costs generated by crime.

The causes of criminality could be the result of an unsafe and dysfunctional home environment during childhood, faulty teaching, and/or faulty learning during childhood, environmental and situational factors outside the home, childhood traumatic experiences, boredom, and individual temperament. It is very difficult to pinpoint which cause is the most influential because it probably varies from individual to individual.

The perspective presented in this material is that criminality has in its background, the following:

- Poor nurturing received in the family of origin
- Poor attachment capability
- Poor social skills
- Selfishness
- Impulsivity
- A mind that has failed to integrate and internalize the following values: Family, Education, Career/Work, and Community. This type of mental frame is also void of the following virtues: Altruism, Honor, Temperance, Dignity, Respect, Order, Sincerity, Justice, Prudence, and Tranquility
- In modern societies, drug and alcohol abuse have brought an increase in criminality.

Values and virtues are rational elements. Criminals are by no means rational people. They are chaotic in their thinking, disorganized, and confused regarding their perspective on life. The criminal frame of mind presents evidence of severe internal deficiency, which is the result of a lack of proper guidance, education, supervision, and teaching that should have been implemented during early childhood.

Criminality, potentially, starts in homes where drugs and alcohol abuse are prevalent, where child abuse is being perpetrated, where parents are abusive toward each other, and where the presence of an attachment disorder between family members exists.

The University of California's Department of Criminality in their work on "Crime and Criminality," stated that the United States is currently facing an overwhelming rise in crime. In that same work, it is also pointed out that crime increased by 40 percent between the years 1970 and 1990, with financial costs going from $12.3 billion in 1970 to $74.3 billion in 1990. Therefore, crime represents a direct attack against the nation's economy, and it also attacks its system of values and virtues, causing the entire society to be caught up in very serious moral and spiritual decay.

## The Birth of a Criminal

A child is born without being given the option to choose what kind of family to be born into. If the unborn child were given a choice as to which family to be born into, chances are a lot of babies who are in this world now, would not be. The problem is that many of those who have become parents were not ready to have children. Children demand a lot from their caretakers, and they can be extremely challenging to the ability people have to provide appropriate care. Who are the parents referred to here? They are the boys and girls who meet in life, then fall in love, but due to lack of proper maturation, do not possess the cognitive and emotional capability to assume the responsibilities of having their own family. In fact, even their preparedness to become intimately involved with another person is very poor, much less have children. They have underlying issues such as traumatic experiences in their background, which were never addressed to a level conducive to an enhanced sense of wellbeing. They never developed adequate communication skills to be able to discuss relationship issues and family problems without increased frustration and anger. These are the people who, too often, engage in screaming matches, pushing, and shoving, which in many cases end up escalating into more severe physical actions such as slapping, punching, and strangling. Their household is in constant turmoil, and it is chaotic. And babies do not do well in turmoil and chaos.

Other couples, in addition to poor communication skills and unaddressed underlying issues, are also engaged in some form of chemical substance abuse, such as illicit drugs, alcoholism, and/or prescription drug abuse. People who are abusing or are already dependent on drugs and alcohol, should not bring babies into their lives. Babies do not do well in a home where chemical substance abuse is going on, due to the potential that drugs have to completely disrupt the home environment. Whatever personal issues individuals might have, will always become exacerbated when chemical substance is in the milieu.

Attachment disorder, as mentioned above, is another condition that must be taken into consideration here. People with unaddressed trauma in their background, and poor communication skills, with or without chemical substance abuse, tend to have very poor social skills and also have very poor bonding capabilities. Children, who grow up in an environment of emotional detachment, have greater chances of engaging in criminal behaviors. Detachment causes the inability to bond and children growing up in this type of family dynamics, usually grow up with a very serious nurturing deficiency. Experts agree that nurturing, or the lack of it, is an influential factor in generating potential for a life of crime.

Emotional detachment, lack of affection, and stressed parents all cooperate for parental inability to offer their children the necessary conditions for adequate human growth. Deficient human growth always proves itself to be very problematic once the individual is at adulthood because the individual was not provided the appropriate conditions to be able to develop efficient strategies for daily living.

Deficient strategies mean that the person is incapacitated in the following areas:

- Satisfactorily functioning within a familial system
- Consistency in his education
- Keeping stable employment
- Controlling impulsivity
- Implementing adequate self-care skills.
- Finding a point of balance mentally: avoiding chaotic thinking and poor thought processing.
- Experiencing a sense of personal satisfaction, causing him to always feel unfulfilled
- Adequately caring for self and others.

Individuals who did not receive adequate care during childhood go through life, quite often, feeling unloved and uncared for. This constitutes their most harmful deficiency. To feel loved and cared for is an essential element for all humans. This is a foundational factor because it characterizes how people relate to themselves and others. Therefore, those individuals who were not treated with love and care during childhood were not provided with an opportunity to learn how to love and care for themselves or others. They do not care much for themselves, and they certainly do not care to contribute to the well-being of others. And they don't care if they victimize others or not. They exist in a vacuum, and from their perspective, nothing matters, nothing is important, nothing is sacred, not even life itself. This can be considered to be the recipe for criminality.

The value of life can only be found in true love. Only that which people love becomes important to them, and that includes their own lives and the lives of others. Criminals are destitute of the ability to love themselves or others, and that could be the primary condition leading them to a life of crime.

Human beings need to be loved and nurtured, even before birth. For them to receive adequate care, be provided a safe environment, be protected, be loved, and be held and hugged is to facilitate personal growth, and in this way, increase the chances of a more efficient functioning person. This quality of care is primarily the responsibility of parents and/or guardians, who should take the first initiative toward making sure that the child feels loved and wanted.

To love and to be loved is a matter of a learning experience, and that must begin in the maternal uterus. All babies are born gentle, incapable of acts of aggression, dependent on responsible adults for survival, for education and to be helped toward directing their energy in the right direction, as they move from early childhood to their adolescent years. Parents ought to conduct themselves as leaders and not push or drag their children along the way by use of forceful means. Children, as special, need their parents or guardians to lead by example. When parents find themselves using forceful means, it is a sign that the educational, and guidance process and acting as role models have suffered a collapse somewhere. Parents must be insightful to determine where they have committed an error so that appropriate corrections can be made.

When parents consistently fail to provide guidance and education to their children and often expose the children to their chaos and inconsistencies, and while blaming the children for failure to comply with their rules and regulations, they are no longer acting as positive role models. They have failed in their leadership role, and have failed to provide a good example, causing a breakdown in the dynamics of communication between them and their children. The most efficient approach to decrease the chances of people leaving their family of origin, and going into a life of crime in society is to have parental skills improved as follows:

- Parents need to have enhanced skills in leadership and must have the know-how in family administration. They have to be emotionally and psychologically healthy, and capable of functioning within the dynamics of familial relationships.
- They need improved skills in how to teach, guide and educate.

- They need to be informed regarding the importance of nurturing, caring, and supervising their children.
- Parents must be educated on how to differentiate between the importance of bonding and their parental authority. If parents can have increased skills in how to motivate bonding formation between themselves and their children, they will find out that authority is actually a secondary element in familial systems. Authority is a necessary element in secular systems, which the family is not. The only authority that is consistent with family life is that which emanates from love, nurturing behaviors, patience, tolerance, and compassion. Whenever authority becomes necessary, it must be implemented not by power and control, but by excellent role modeling, and a consistent pattern of communication from the parents to their children.

# Criminal Intention

Criminality does not constitute a pattern of conduct that happens purely by accident, it is not a matter of having an opportunity, and neither is it triggered by some type of pre-existent motivation to break the law. All criminal acts require an intention before being committed. The intention is then a key element. All criminals are opportunists, preferring to act in darkness and without any eyewitnesses. However, even the best of opportunities could not lead an individual to transgress the law, unless an intention exists internally.

Most people are faced with an opportunity to commit a crime just about every day of their lives. There is the opportunity to drive over the speed limit, there is the opportunity to physically assault someone due to anger, and there is the opportunity to take something that does not belong to us. So, it is not opportunity that leads people to commit a crime, not primarily. It is not the fact that they have a need such as driving over the speed limit because they are late going to work. It is not the opportunity to take someone else's money because they may be hungry, but it is the presence of an intention to act criminally and lacking the capability to control the internal impulses deriving from such an intention.

Let's use suicide as an example: many individuals experience suicidal thoughts, but they are considered to be at a high risk to harm themselves when they report having an intention and/or a plan. Opportunities are everywhere, such as knives to cut themselves with, medications to overdose on, ropes and/or cords to hang oneself with, and bridges to jump from, but unless there is an intention, the chances of a suicidal gesture are greatly decreased.

Criminality also requires the concept of an intention if there is going to be an attempt. The intention is the result of thought processing, and in the case of the actual intent to commit a crime, the thought processing is of very low-quality, showing evidence that it is completely destitute of virtues and values. The thinking is marked by poor judgment, no skills in making decisions, lack of altruism, no personal responsibility, and complete disregard for personal accountability. This type of thinking is influenced by selfishness, greed, rebellion, impulsivity, and carelessness.

Human behavior is a direct result of internal disposition. People cannot act without commands from the inside. Two essential elements can be considered to be important factors in every human initiative: (1) Thoughts, and (2) Intentionality. This influence of thoughts and intention is also a factor emphasized in spirituality, and we read in Hebrews 4:12,

*"For the word of God is living and powerful, and sharper than any two-edged sword, piercing even to the division of soul and spirit, and of joints and marrow, and is a discerner of the **thoughts and intents of the heart**."*
Criminals are people who lack insight into their thoughts

and intentions, and that is one reason they tend to act impulsively.

Thoughts are important, as they contain intentions. I could say that thoughts are impregnated with intentions, and they make a man what he is, as we read in Proverbs 23:7,

"For as he thinks in his heart, so *is* he."

Criminal intention consists of an individual considering his criminal act by contemplating and assessing the pros and cons, to arrive at some kind of conclusion about where and how to commit a criminal act. In this case, whenever the conclusion favors the perpetration of a crime, it serves the purpose of solidifying the intention. Next, the criminal mind begins planning how to carry out the established intent. Motivation and opportunity are factors, but secondary to intentionality.

In the process of an individual considering "to be or not to be a criminal," and "to do or not to do a crime," values and virtues are the only elements that have the potential to maintain the person within the boundaries of integrity. There is nothing else that can help an individual to maintain emotional and cognitive balance outside of values and virtues.

Criminals live meaningless lives. Values and virtues are representatives of the real meaning of life, and they have the potential to stabilize life and nurture wholesomeness. They are essential for a high-quality life, supporting the will to live, the disposition to belong, and the desire to help and be cooperative with others. They strengthen the human self and generate the will to care for family, others, and the community. These elements are completely strange to criminals, who would rather thrive in treachery and in creating havoc.

Criminals reject the idea of making a living by virtuous means such as being industrious, responsible, placing value on a career/work, and diligence. They are unable to establish intents that are validated by any virtue or value. Their predisposition to crime is not based on low intelligence or cognitive deficits, but due to very low self-care skills, poor judgment, and poor decision-making capability.

Criminals can be very articulate, very smart, and high functioning, such as the politician who bribes and who takes bribes or the businessman who will cheat and cause their business partner to suffer great losses.

The decision to commit a crime, for so many individuals, is made purely based on impulsivity because, in that given moment, they completely ignore the consequences of their actions. Impulsive types of behavior are destitute of the competence to care for oneself. Impulsive individuals do not possess the competence to make decisions to avoid legal and/or financial problems. People who maintain a consistent pattern of initiatives, in ways that keep bringing the same costly results over and over again, demonstrate that they have very poor skills in realistically handling life.

Life is not forgiving, and it requires facts. Life demands that decisions be made in a timely and realistic manner. Therefore, one must be competent to avoid the consequences that life brings. Impulsive people live trapped in the here and now, unable and unwilling to consider the negative consequences reaped yesterday and are also unable to appropriately plan for tomorrow.

## Three Groups of People

People, with reference to criminality, can be divided into three different groups, with the first group of people being formed by those who are not concerned with themselves or others. This group reaches its lowest point morally and spiritually when they no longer care about the idea of being arrested by the police and then imprisoned. That could be said to be almost the point of no return for so many. Because, again, they are the type of people that are unable to properly evaluate negative consequences, and then change course toward more beneficial outcomes.

The second group is formed by individuals who, on occasion, have thoughts of committing some form of crime, such as taking money that is not theirs or acting dishonestly to profit, but who do not follow up for fear of consequences. However, they would, possibly, act criminally if they could be sure they would get away with it. So, fear of the consequences becomes their restraining power.

The third group is formed by those possessing a reasonable degree of mental and emotional stability. They are competent in making quality decisions and are highly moral and spiritual people. They have learned to be responsible for their actions. They are invested in themselves, in their families, and in their community. They may experience thoughts of wanting to break boundaries but are well capable of exercising control over their thoughts. This group needs to grow in number because society, today, is in great need of this type of individual. Let's propose one more argument in favor of beliefs, values, and virtues. What kind of people are criminals? Are they the type that could be said to be personally responsible for their actions? Are they concerned for others? Are they prudent? Are they altruistic? We know that the answer to these questions is no, they are not! If criminals had been taught these virtues from childhood and into adulthood, chances are, they would not be living a life of crime, with very few exceptions.

Criminals are to the family and the community what cancer is to the human body. A cancer cell is a disorganized cell, isolated from other cells in the human body, which, to survive, needs to devour the healthy cells around it, thus engaging itself in a process that has the potential to destroy the entire human body. Cancer in the human body is a problem that demands immediate, aggressive, and efficient intervention to have it completely removed. Criminality, without efficient intervention, has the potential to cause society exactly what cancer does to the physical body, for in the process of time, criminality does have the potential to destroy society. Police intervention is an absolute necessity, and police personnel must be well-trained, and must not be hesitant when dealing with criminals. I believe that police officers must be able to do whatever they have to do, legally, to bring criminals under their custody. Criminals, when the crime calls for it, need to be apprehended so that they are no longer able to commit other crimes. To firmly and consistently combat crime is the responsibility of the authorities.

## The Value of Self-control.

One common initiative to control human behavior is the making of laws. Laws are extremely important because without laws there would be complete chaos. Laws do serve the purpose of protecting society from those who have the disposition to cause harm to others, and it ensures that transgressors are properly punished. However, the legal system, just like the individuals who write and continue to revise the legal code, is not perfect. Imperfection is unable to create perfection. If the laws and their enforcement were perfect, there wouldn't be any transgression of the law, such as illicit drug use, driving under the influence, robbing banks, acts of aggression and violence, etc.

Laws must be respected and obeyed, which is a response that requires individuals to have the internal capacity to do so. When individuals break the law, we have in their transgression the evidence that these individuals have failed to comply, and the main explanation for their failure to comply is their faulty internal frame. Furthermore, this failure to comply is not the result of individuals not knowing specific laws, but rather due to the following:

- They do not possess the internal ability to be able to establish a better course of direction.
- They are individuals who are unwilling to obey the law because they don't see any value in complying with the law.
- In their faulty perception of life, they see more benefit in breaking the law than obeying it.

- Their field vision is distorted, and the expectations they have been able to establish are lacking in integrity. Therefore, they are unable to provide for themselves.
- And, they have developed the thought patterns of a criminal, and to live the life of a criminal is all they know.

These reasons are indicative of the fact that they are internally disorganized and deficient. Laws do serve another purpose, which is that they force individuals to consider their actions and to think twice before they act in any way that could possibly lead to transgressing the law. Those individuals who are capable of doing so, are regarded as being responsible citizens, law-abiding, and competent in making decisions. These are individuals equipped with a reasonable degree of capability in:

- Personal responsibility
- Making sound judgment
- Possessing an adequate degree of self-care skills
- Having a well-defined set of beliefs that they live by, including religious and cultural beliefs.
- Having family, community, patriotic and spiritual values help them to maintain a more stable lifestyle.

These are individuals who have developed the ability to evaluate and measure the consequences of their actions. In Galatians 6:7-10, the spiritual principle establishes that,

*"Do not be deceived, God is not mocked; for whatever a man sows, that he will also reap. For he who sows to his flesh will of the flesh reap corruption, but he who sows to the Spirit will of the Spirit reap everlasting life. And let us not grow weary while doing good, for in due season we shall reap if we do not lose heart. Therefore, as we have opportunity, let us do good to all, especially to those who are of the household of faith."* And, they also understand accountability, as Saint Paul writes to the Romans, saying,

*"So, then each of us shall give account of himself to God."* They understand that they are also accountable to the Law of the Land, and to mankind as a whole.

People can prove to be dysfunctional in many different aspects of life and may demonstrate an inability to self-regulate well. They struggle to maintain a stable lifestyle, are deficient regarding personal responsibility, have inadequate judgment, and decision-making is not a part of their way of thinking, requiring skills they do not possess. As a result of this three-fold deficit, they are always at risk of taking unlawful initiatives. These risky initiatives are chemical substance abuse, aggression, and violence, or living a life of more serious criminal behaviors. Dysfunctional homes are chaotic as a rule and tend to raise cognitively chaotic individuals.

In order to have increased compliance with the law, each individual needs the following:

- He must believe that obeying the law is necessary, and even beneficial to himself and his community.
- He must be willing to comply.
- He must develop a virtuous perception of the legal system by fully understanding its value and its benefits to the family and community.
- He must be able to see the integrity of the law and its purpose for families, the local community, and the entire society.
- He must be able to live harmoniously with himself and others.
- He must be able to cope with life soberly.
- He must experience peace within himself.
- He must become fully responsible for all his actions.

## Moral and Spiritual Codes

This internal capability to comply with the laws of the land, and to live harmoniously with all the established cultural norms of society, has to be the result of an education process started in early childhood. Parents are responsible for the laying of this foundation, and when they fail, law enforcement may have to intervene to deal with situations that could have been avoided. Poor parenting represents a great disservice to human beings, and consequently to society.

Saint Paul, in Ephesians 6:4, provides parents with the following advisement:

*"And you, fathers, do not provoke your children to wrath, but bring them up in the training and admonition of the Lord."*

In Colossians 3:21, the same Apostle Paul states:

*"Fathers, do not provoke your children, lest they become discouraged."*

Parents must understand that their homes must be a place in which all family members are being nurtured and helped to become functional human beings. Parents ought to want their homes and family to be blessed, and not cursed. A dysfunctional home is dysfunctional for a reason, and that reason is never a good one. In the Book of Proverbs 1:33, we read:

*"The curse of the Lord is on the house of the wicked, but He blesses the home of the just."*

Who are the just? The just are people who understand they must provide their children with the following:

- an environment in which there is physical and emotional safety

- An environment of love, care, nurture, and appropriate supervision
- Just parents understand what their role is within the home, and can provide even sacrificial parenting, when necessary.

Albert Bandura (1962), the author of Social Learning Theory, and who has written works on social foundations of thoughts and actions, stated that children learn primarily by the actions of the parents, and secondarily by what parents say. The actions must always be consistent with what is said. According to Bandura, role modeling is a crucial element in child-rearing.

Parents do require, from the children, an appropriate response to their determinations. Responses, from children, must be an initiative from within each individual, and it requires a capability that the individual may either possess or not. If parents keep on providing a child with a set of instructions, and the child continues to act by disregarding the instructions received, then the conclusion of the parents might be that they have to take further action. Usually, the action that is taken is some form of punishment/disciplining, when truthfully, they should increase education, intensifying the teaching process in the attempt to promote better understanding regarding established parental expectations. And, if this fails, then there must be punishment/discipline.

The legal system does use a more direct approach when dealing with transgressors. It takes the actions that are necessary when dealing with the defiant person: it does indeed punish, but punishment does not work the same for everyone. That is, not everybody responds in the same way. Some people improve, and others grow worse.

When the legal system or parents are faced with a situation in which punishment is the measure to be used, it is an indication that the individual being dealt with is lacking the internal ability to properly respond to the situation, and now he will be dealt with by use of force or infliction of pain.

The use of force is in direct opposition to the principles of making choices. Choices should be the result of good judgment, which should be the result of proper parental leadership in providing:

- Supervision
- Guidance
- Instruction
- Training by role modeling, and,
- Education.

The individual who was not the recipient of virtuous parenting will come to the age of accountability and will find himself dealing with external demands yet lacking the internal structure to adequately respond to them. He will find himself falling short of the external expectations imposed by others and the environment around him. And, when having to cope with people, rules, regulations, and environmental demands, his internal deficiency will manifest itself. This inability to adequately respond to others, situations, and circumstances, can cause life to strike him as being extremely difficult. He finds himself unable to progress, his frustration level becomes elevated, and he becomes easily irritated, and could become labile at times. His problem is that internally he is not in control of his thoughts, emotions, and volition.

What is parental influence? It is one of the most important roles human beings can perform in life. Nothing is more important than being a parent. It is a huge error of judgment when people regard work and paying bills as a priority over raising their children. Having a job and paying bills is a very important part of it, but at a secondary level of importance when compared to teaching and educating them. Therefore, raising children requires the highest level of responsibility compared to any other that a human being may accept in this life, and it represents the highest calling. No other activity in life should require more training and preparation than parenting.

The human person is given power and possesses the ability to make decisions, and for an individual to make quality decisions, he needs to be able to judge, but if the judgment is poor, consequently, decisions will also be poor. Poor decisions bring negative consequences, which are usually punitive actions.

A very important part of decision-making is to be able to say no or yes, depending on the situation. For anyone to say either yes or no, he must be able to determine internally if the situation that he is now facing is one to say no or yes to, and such a determination cannot be made without appropriate judgment.

A judge, when ruling on a particular case, takes all evidence presented into consideration, and then makes his judgment based on the determinations of the Code of Law. Individuals need to develop a code of conduct with the support of diligent parenting. This code of conduct becomes an inherent part of their thinking.

The ability to make appropriate judgments in daily situations, to determine if it requires a yes or a no, is of extreme importance in the prevention and treatment of chemical substance abuse, and other problematic behaviors, including criminality.

What is it that individuals are supposed to use to correctly judge daily situations? They have a need to develop a code of morality or conduct, and they must also integrate and internalize basic spiritual principles.

This process of developing an internal code of conduct is foundational and must be initiated by capable parents. Both morality and spirituality must be established during the early stages of life, and can most definitely help individuals to have increased skills in how to:

- Better care for themselves
- Be better connected to others i.e., family, neighbors, friends, and co-workers
- Develop adequate personal boundaries, to be able to preserve a healthy sense of individual identity
- Learn to live responsibly toward self and others
- Value family life and interaction
- Recognize and value true friendship
- Value and appreciate their community, having the insight that what helps their community is also helpful to them
- Be aware of and be reliant on God's help.

## External Regulation

When the process of building the foundation of the human person is defective, it incurs decreased internal capability, and the chances for external intervention are automatically increased.

The following are common examples of external intervention:

- Law enforcement represents a primary level of external intervention. It is very effective in restraining human behavior, and when individuals are unable to self-regulate, then, law enforcement comes onto the scene. Law enforcement intervention is, contrary to the perception of a lot of people, good and necessary. Law enforcement represents the external intervention that could save a marriage, in the case of domestic abuse/violence, and it could save a life, in the case of one driving under the influence. Law enforcement could save lives by removing individuals who have evil intentions from the streets, therefore serving also the purpose of preserving the integrity of families and their communities. Law enforcement is a constant reminder of consequences. However, criminality, chemical substance abuse, bullying, shoplifting, aggression, and violence are all marked basically by a great degree of impulsivity. Impulsive people never consider consequences, and they are poor thinkers.

Compliance with the law is for people who are rational, who have values, who are virtuous, and who have learned to respect the laws because they are capable of measuring consequences.

- Lawyers
- District attorneys
- Department of Human Services
- Judges
- City jail, county jail, and State/Federal prisons

The need for external intervention is an indication of internal deficits. Education must be provided to improve internal capability, so there can be a decrease in the need for external intervention. Education must be provided promptly, to serve as effective prevention.

# Conclusion

Law enforcement personnel are servants of the Most-High God, and so are those who put laws in place. They should not create laws only for the sake of mankind on earth, but also because it is their responsibility before the Holy Father in Heaven. According to Romans 13:1-2: *"Let every soul be subject to the governing authorities. For there is no authority except from God, and the authorities that exist are appointed by God. Therefore, whoever resists the authority resists the ordinance of God, and those who resist will bring judgment on themselves."*

God does hold people responsible for how they use their authority. God had a reason to provide people with authority, and with the Code of Law. The three Abrahamic religions which are Jewish, Islamic, and Christianity are deeply influenced by the Ten Commandments. A person cannot study jurisprudence in most nations of the world, and not take into consideration the Mosaic Law. God, by giving Moses the Ten Commandments, has deeply established His moral and spiritual principles into the reality of men. God has created an entire structure, and mankind cannot escape it.

People have a choice to acknowledge God or not, and they can certainly choose to serve Him or not, but escape God's system, they cannot. Sooner or later, everyone will have to give account to Him. God knows best, and He knew what was best for mankind, probably millions of years before mankind ever existed. He knew that without law and order, society cannot survive. God wants people to have guidelines to live by. He knows that without a sense of direction, mankind will be morally and spiritually disoriented. Yes, if any human being wants to go to Heaven, he/she needs to follow the principles of God's word, but this one truth remains, mankind cannot survive without law and order, and the Code of Law must regulate morality.

When God provides instruction it is because He knows mankind needs to have boundaries. He gave laws to men, so they could teach these laws which, in reality, are principles of life. God is concerned with families, and He is concerned with each generation of mankind. He motivated parents to teach their children, so that one spiritually and morally safe generation would pass their knowledge down to the next generation, and that is what we read in Deuteronomy 6:6-7,

*"And these words which I command you today shall be in your heart. You shall teach them diligently to your children and shall talk of them when you sit in your*

*house, when you walk by the way, when you lie down, and when you rise up. You shall bind them as a sign on your hand, and they shall be as frontlets between your eyes. You shall write them on the doorposts of your house and on your gates."*

In Joshua 22:5, we read,

*"But take careful heed to do the commandment and the law which Moses the servant of the Lord commanded you, to love the Lord your God, to walk in all His ways, to keep His commandments, to hold fast to Him, and to serve Him with all your heart and with all your soul."*

In this text we have God motivating people toward being law-abiding, and if each generation would be diligent regarding the laws of God, criminality would not have a future on the earth. To be a law-abiding person is not something we do to go to Heaven, but we do it so we can live well on earth. There is safety in keeping the law of God, and the law of the land. Parents should teach their children to obey the law because it can save them and their children a lot of headaches.

An act of the will caused Lucifer to come out from under the kingship and Lordship of God, and it takes an act of the will to establish divine sovereignty over our lives. Why is this so important? Because it determines what influences people's lives, whether to live according to God's principles, or Lucifer's.

In I Chronicles 29:11-12, we read:

*"Yours, O Lord, is the greatness, the power and the glory, The victory and the majesty; for all that is in heaven and in earth is Yours; yours is the kingdom, O Lord, and You are exalted as head over all. Both riches and honor come from You, and You reign over all. In Your hand is power and might; In Your hand it is to make great and to give strength to all."*

These two verses give us information on how people can live safely on the earth, both morally and spiritually. Criminality can be addressed in two ways: we can use biblical principles, and we can also use the Code of Law. Parents, clergy, and teachers ought to make use of biblical principles, and law enforcement personnel must make use of the Code of Laws.

In Psalm 103:19, we read:

*"The Lord has established His throne in heaven, and His kingdom rules over all."*

To think that the first crime ever committed was an attempt against the throne of God. What was Lucifer thinking? The only explanation I have is that he became extremely delusional, and his delusional state was deeply influenced by grandiose. I refer to that as the grandiosity of all grandiose because it attacked the highest seat in the entire universe: God's throne. That was not such an uncommon crime in the times of the kings of the earth, but to attempt to overturn God's throne? In fact, it was insanity even to attempt it against the throne of a human king, and many died trying, now imagine going against the throne of God!

This delusion is set in the heart of criminality, causing some people to think that they can live their lives ignoring and having contempt for the element of authority. No condition fits the statement "against the tide," better than criminality. Criminals are going against the tide, and the worse aspect of it is that, in many cases, before they are stopped, too many innocent people have been hurt, and even killed.

Thoughts to consider:

- The call of law enforcement to establish "law and order," is not just an earthly call, but it is also a Heavenly call (Romans 13:1).
- As lawlessness increases, so does the resistance to the presence of law enforcement, but law enforcement personnel are servants of mankind and of God, so they must not give up.
- They must perform their duties with honor, pride, and love, knowing that to "save a life could mean the same as to save a world" (Anonymous).

- Law enforcement personnel must always keep in mind that what they do is not just part of having a carrier, but it is a calling of a Higher Order, and today it has become an urgent necessity.
- Be proud of what you do!

Law enforcement personnel are the guardians of rules and regulations within society. Life, without rules and regulations, would certainly become chaotic. This truth cannot be neglected by politicians because they might consider it to be too conservative, and conservative folks should not neglect it either. Just because a person votes conservative does not mean that she/he is a firm believer in the importance of rules and regulations. Every place of business has rules and regulations, and they are so important that they even post them on their front door. Rules and regulations are like a guiding light, and they establish behavioral boundaries. Every household should have well-established rules and regulations if they expect family members to behave properly. Families which do not have established parameters by which family members ought to behave are more likely to be disrupted when compared with those families that do. In the same way that we need rules and regulations for places of business, and for households, so we also need them for the streets.

People cannot be allowed to think that they, when out in the streets, can do as they please. Why not? Because we know that there are people whose ideas of having fun and enjoying themselves could involve trespassing on someone's private property or causing damages to property, and even could put at risk the safety of others.

People need to be regulated, and legally regulated. And, in the same way that rules and regulations in households, and places of business must be enforced, they must also be enforced out in the streets. To have rules and regulations and not enforce them represents a waste of time and effort. If rules and regulations are not to be followed, then we must come up with some other ways to regulate people. And what would that be? The system of rewards, maybe? Maybe we should start giving hugs to those who are physically aggressive, to those who have homicidal thoughts, those who are set on the idea of being thieves, and those who are sexual molesters of children, and hopefully, they will reconsider, and change their ways. Is that it? This is what the liberal politicians want, which is to reward criminals and not be so harsh on them, trying to convince the world that the discriminatory and judgmental attitudes of society are the elements that have led them to their criminality.

People have options on how to live their lives, and individuals are autonomous in their decision-making. Saint Paul, in Romans 14:12 wrote:

"So, then each of us shall give account of himself to God."

And finally, the Code of Law, and rules and regulations in general as it applies to households, places of business, or the streets, should not be processed as liberal or conservative elements, but it must be embraced by all as a system of support for the human person, and to enforce them is the only pathway we have to establish and maintain law and order."

# Sources

1. New King James Version
2. Wycliffe Bible
3. New Life Version
4. Adler, A. (1998). Understanding Life. Center City, MN: Hazelden
5. Peterson, J.V., & Nisenholz, B (1999). Orientation to Counseling (4th Ed.) Boston: Allyn & bacon
6. Vacc, N.A. & Loesch, L.C, (2000). Professional Orientation to Counseling (3rd Ed.) Philadelphia, PA: Taylor & Francis
7. Corey, G. (1996). Theory and Practice of counseling and Psychotherapy (5th Ed.). Pacific Grove, CA: Brooks/Cole
8. Peterson, C., & Seligman, M.E.P. (2004). Character Strengths and Virtues: A handbook and Classification. Oxford University Press.
9. Bandura, A. (1962). Social Learning Through Imitation. University of Nebraska Press: Lincoln, NE.
10. Bandura, A. (1975). Social Learning & Personality Development. Holt, Rinehart & Winston, Inc: NJ.

11. Meichenbaum, D.H. (1977). Cognitive and behavior modification. New York: Plenum.

12. O.C. Simonton, (1992). Getting Well Again. New York: Bantam Books

13. Kiev, Ari. Magic, Faith, and healing. New York: The Free Press, 1969.

14. Pelletier, K.R., (1977). Mind as Healer, Mind as Slayer. New York: Dell Publishing

15. Oxford English Dictionary: Oxford University Press.

16. The University of California. Crime and criminality. Department of Criminality. Crime and Criminality, Chapter 16. Books on Line.

17. https://simplypsychology.org/maslow

Made in the USA
Monee, IL
19 September 2023

42932235R00149